HOW SMART WOMEN ACHIEVE BIG GOALS

HOW SMART WOMEN ACHIEVE BIG GOALS

Motivation To Focus and Follow Through With Your Life Dreams

ALLISON J. FOSKETT, M.Sc.

iUniverse, Inc.
Bloomington

HOW SMART WOMEN ACHIEVE BIG GOALS
Motivation To Focus and Follow Through With Your Life Dreams

Allison Foskett, M.Sc., CCC.
Edmonton, Alberta
www.goal-setting-motivation.com
ali@goal-setting-motivation.com
allisonfoskett@live.ca

iUniverse books may be ordered through booksellers or by contacting:

iUniverse
1663 Liberty Drive
Bloomington, IN 47403
www.iuniverse.com
1-800-Authors (1-800-288-4677)

ISBN: 978-1-4620-6438-0 (sc)
ISBN: 978-1-4620-6439-7 (ebk)

Printed in the United States of America

iUniverse rev. date: 02/25/2012

ACKNOWLEDGEMENTS

I would like to acknowledge all my friends, family, clients, mentors and supervisors who inspired me to be true to my own goals in writing and completing my first book.

Thank you to: Norm Ammoun for his many book cover designs including the final book cover, and all his support and patience in this process; to Gail Kearns, from To Press and Beyond (http://www.topressandbeyond.com/), for her advice and editing assistance with this manuscript; to Dan Poynter, (http://www.parapublishing.com/sites/para/about/danpoynter.cfm) for his guidance and advice while at his dinner party and seminars in London, Ontario, and Edmonton Alberta. His books and online resources have eased this process greatly. Thank you to the women who allowed me to interview them for their stories on how they achieved their life dreams and goals; and to HARO (Help a Reporter—http://www.helpareporter.com/) for assisting me in reaching these women.

DISCLAIMER

The purpose of this book is to provide women with information, insights and new perspectives on dreaming big, setting goals and following them through to completion. This book is intended to educate, empower and entertain readers. The authors and publisher(s) will not be held liable nor responsible to any person, group of persons, company or entity with respect to alleged losses, damages or other reported problems that are caused directly or indirectly from reading the information within this book.

This book is not meant to be a comprehensive account of all information or research ever published on goal setting, motivation, achievement and so forth. Instead, this book offers information that is a reflection of the author's personal research, interests, and creative understanding of the subject matter.

The author cannot guarantee anyone that reading or following the information in this book will enable them to achieve their dreams and goals. There are many complex variables in a person's life that affects how successful they will become as they work towards achieving their life goals. Achieving a life dream or goal is often times hard work, and it takes time. Due to the volume of information in this book, it is possible that this book may have typographical mistakes or content that is not completely accurate. As a result, this book, and the information contained within this book should only be considered general guideline as opposed to prescriptive rules or instructions. If you do not wish to abide by the above information, please return this book and request a full refund.

TABLE OF CONTENTS

INTRODUCTION

THE SPARK THAT IGNITED MY JOURNEY

> Books were my pass to personal freedom. I learned to read at age three, and soon discovered there was a whole world to conquer that went beyond our farm in Mississippi.
> -Oprah

Do you remember what sparked your interest in achieving big goals? What started it all for you? I can remember in my eighth grade coming across a copy of the book, *Think and Grow Rich* by Napoleon Hill. I looked at it and thought it seemed very interesting, but I actually only read the table of contents. Perhaps conceptually speaking, that was all I was ready for at such a young age. I remember thinking to myself that many of the chapters, such as "Desire," "Faith," and "Persistence," all sounded quite magical in nature. This brief encounter sparked something deep inside of me—perhaps hope for my future. A seed was planted, one that I would eventually come to nurture in the future. Somehow, I had the idea within my head that anything was possible to achieve in life if you had the persistence, determination, and the rest of Napoleon Hill's ingredients.

I must admit, however, that it wasn't until I listened to another audio program, Anthony Robbins' "30 Days to Personal Power," that I was completely set on fire! Finding this resource was definitely what hooked me for life. I can remember being so intrigued by the titles of the audio cassettes that included, "The Goal-Setting Workshop" and "The Driving Force." When I began listening to these tapes, I remember feeling exhilarated with all the incredible insights I was learning. I couldn't help but ask myself, *Why didn't we learn this stuff in school?* In fact, I realized that living a life of the status quo bored me to death so much that I would skip classes in high school to go home and voraciously read personal development books. I found within myself this newly created "buzz," a profound sense of excitement and passion that would fill the background of my life forever. To this day, the original spark that ignited my passion is still alive and strong. I'm constantly devouring books and audio programs on goal setting and achievement.

> *Everyone has inside him a piece of good news. The good news is that you don't know how great you can be. How much you can love. What you can accomplish. And what your potential is.*
>
> *-Anne Frank*

By my early twenties, I knew without a doubt that I was going to embark upon a career that enabled me to help others achieve their goals and make life changes. Completing my graduate studies in psychology became a must because I was constantly itching to learn more about what the research demonstrated on human behaviour, change, and motivation. For the past decade, my focus has been counselling and coaching individuals through both personal and career transitions. I've worked with college and university students, adults, executives, seniors, and just about anyone looking to make life changes and achieve goals. What emerged from years of counselling others and listening to their stories was a compelling desire to research their problems and challenges that they encountered, while trying to achieve their goals. For me, it's as though I encounter important mysteries that I become intensely curious about and feel compelled to help my clients solve. Being the voracious reader that I am, I would set out to read as many books and articles as possible on the various problems that my clients encountered. Whether a person had issues with her goals, motivation, relationships, health, career, spirituality, or self-esteem, it didn't matter to me, because they all interested me.

Over time, however, I noticed that I became particularly interested in, not only a person's motivation to achieve her goals, but the entire *process* of setting goals and seeing them through to completion. I noticed that many changes that a person wanted to make were often held back due to lack of motivation or the ability to stay motivated over the long term. It was a great topic to tackle, because *everybody* could always use more motivation in at least one area of life. In addition to researching specific problems, I began to learn more about the process of change, motivation, and how to actually follow through with goals over time. I learned about the stages of change and began to apply these stages to goal setting and achievement. A lot of goal—setting has to do with one's ability to make concrete changes over time.

As I began to learn more about the process of becoming motivated, making life changes, and achieving goals, I found that I had the desire to capture and highlight information that was especially valuable. I was interested in developing a fresh perspective that was based on a concrete process, one that others could easily understand and apply to her own life changes and motivation to achieve her goals. This is essentially what this book is all about—giving you a process that you can use to help you make changes and achieve your life goals.

> *If you don't like something, change it.*
> *If you can't change it, change your attitude.*
> *-Maya Angelou*

It's usually easy enough to *start* making life changes and achieving goals. It's easy to get psyched up in the beginning of a new endeavour or pursuit. Perhaps if a person is in a fairly positive stage of her life, these things come a bit more easily. For others, they hit rock bottom in one area of their life, and they are propelled into action with unstoppable motivation. Some individuals become inspired from a coaching session or a seminar they attended. The reality, however, is that our life context, or what is happening in the background of our life, changes over time. Motivation that at one time came easily eventually wanes. Changes that were easy to maintain at one time can become difficult to maintain at other times in our life. Working towards our goals and following through over time with consistent motivation is something that requires a constant renewal of mental perspectives, attitudes, and energy. Over the course of our lifetime, it is safe to say that our goals need consistent bouts of attention, with rejuvenated efforts that are comprised of continually learning lessons and challenges that we've encountered over time. What I'm excited to offer you is a process that will help you set your goals, build unique personal motivation, and maintain the ability to stay motivated and follow through even when times are tough.

WHO SHOULD READ THIS BOOK?

This book was written for smart women who are passionate about their personal development and want more out of life. Given that you've picked up a copy of my book, I know you're on the right track. As you read, you can expect to find truly unique, yet advanced, personal goal-setting motivation that *works.*

THIS BOOK WAS WRITTEN FOR WOMEN WHO ARE:

- Passionate about their personal development (and some might describe them as "obsessed")
- Overly ambitious
- Insatiably thirsty for self-awareness and knowledge
- Busy with life
- Totally savvy
- Impatient with their achievements
- Completely frustrated by the status quo
- Interested in creating long-lasting achievements and changes over the long run as opposed to expecting superficial results in the short term

As you read, I hope that you will experience the following:

- "Ah-ha" moments, "eureka's," and transformational insights that lead to achieving clarity about your future.
- Powerful context and paradigm shifting questions
- Empowering metaphors and analogies

- Unique and empowering life philosophies
- New belief systems that will propel you into unstoppable action
- And finally, overall fresh perspectives on achievement and motivation

I believe that our biggest fear in life is that we will settle for a status-quo lifestyle, and this motivates us to do something about it. I want to help you expand your life context for what is possible. Some of us already have goals, a purpose, and visions for what is possible, but can and do we commit to *living* these dreams that we have for ourself? If you are like me, and you get a "high" off of experiencing "ah-ha" moments, and you are passionate about personal growth and achievement, then you are just the type of woman I'm looking to connect with.

WHAT MAKES THIS BOOK UNIQUE?

Within this book, you will find a comprehensive goal-setting and motivation program that teaches you a *system* or *process* that has been derived from, and in part, is based on the scientific stages of change also known as the Transtheoretical Model of Change (Prochaska, Norcross, & Diclemente, 1994). There is no doubt that achieving life goals requires a series of adjustments and changes: changes in our attitudes and thoughts, our behaviours and habits, and even changes in our environment. This goal-setting and motivation system is one that you can "recycle" and use over and over again *for life*.

What's unique about this goal-setting and motivation program is that it is very comprehensive in nature. Many books focus on getting individuals to outline a detailed action plan and provide instructions to begin taking immediate action steps towards their goals. Unfortunately, in our fast-paced culture, everything is about rushing into action and achieving immediate results. The best examples to support this are individual efforts to go on a financial budget or a healthy diet. Most people start off with high levels of motivation, only to later find their motivation wane. Then, they wonder what is wrong with them. They conclude that they have little self-discipline, that they're lazy or simply not meant to achieve their goals. However, nothing could be further from the truth, because the problem doesn't lie in having a lack of self-discipline or will power. The problem lies in people not taking the time to work through the initial tasks of preparation that are required for developing both short—and long-term motivation. The good news is that there are many concrete exercises or tasks that a person can work through, all of which will address many commitment and motivation issues surrounding the achievement of their goals.

The second piece that many people aren't aware of is that motivation is something a person needs to work on *for life*. It's no different than getting your nutrition. You don't eat a serving of broccoli once, and then find yourself topped up on vitamin C forever. If you want the benefits of eating cruciferous vegetables, you have to eat them often. The same principle applies to success in almost every area of our life, because our success is dependent upon the consistent effort that we invest in our goals on a regular basis. The same rule applies to motivation and following through with achieving your life goals. You will need to constantly address issues of motivation. This book isn't just your typical goal-setting book that tries to superficially inspire and motivate you. I am going to educate you on the tasks that are involved in motivating yourself. You will have a complete process-oriented system that you can apply to develop all your life goals, including your relationships, health, career, finances, and other goals.

Another important and unique concept about this book is that it puts you in the driver's seat. You will be in charge of creating your own personalized motivation, meanings, and insights. What makes this program so valuable is that you will benefit by creating your own unique perspectives, rather than simply absorbing and accepting someone else's perspectives. Instead of passively reading a book where someone is telling you what you should think and what you should do, I'm going to do the opposite. I'm going to provide you with over one hundred dynamic and creative "power" questions to help you gain self-awareness into what your goals are, how to prioritize them, how to develop the motivation behind them, and finally, how to identify your limiting thoughts and behaviours and replace them with personalized substitutes that are meaningful and motivating to you.

BREAKTHROUGHS IN PERSPECTIVES

Throughout the various exercises and corresponding questions in this book, you will notice that whenever possible I list alternative pieces of language to enrich the relevancy and meaningfulness of the exercises. I draw on different pieces of language to help spark your creativity, and I provide you with ways of knowing yourself and what motivates you. The last thing I want to happen is that you take any of the exercises for granted. Some pieces of language or words tend to spark powerful realizations or breakthroughs in perspectives for some people, yet mean nothing to the next person. Likewise, some words conjure up particular images or connotations for one person, while these same words may have a completely different effect on someone else. I've tried to prevent this from happening.

I hope that reading this book is a lively and meaningful experience for you. To do this, you'll notice that in many of the questions, I have tried to use what I refer to as creative tactics to get you thinking in abstract ways about your motivation and goals. I am constantly aiming to increase the number of "ah-ha" moments, insights, or personal breakthroughs that you will experience. I sometimes make comparisons on perspectives and philosophies to encourage you to look at things differently. By asking you a number of different questions and using a variety of different pieces of language, I'm essentially hoping to maximize new ways of thinking and fresh perspectives that are personally constructed by you.

My hope is for you to "own" your own style of goal-setting and your own customized sources of motivation that you will continually develop and modify throughout your life. Identifying and prioritizing your goals and finding ways to continually rejuvenate your motivation, so that you can stay committed to those goals is a challenging task. If you use the program provided in this book, you'll increase your chances of attaining success, and you'll achieve it with greater ease.

HOW YOU WILL BENEFIT FROM READING THIS BOOK

This book will provide you with a unique step-by-step goal-setting and motivation blueprint that will help you construct your own, personalized motivation, mindsets, beliefs, feelings, and behaviours that will drastically increase your chances of *following through* with any ambition.

This is an easy-to-follow *process* that you'll love because of its simplicity and ease. It's so easy that you'll find your goals constantly *evolving*, rather than *dissolving* into lost dreams and memories. How do I accomplish this? The entire program is comprised of over one hundred and fifty creative and dynamic questions that will assist you in the intricate process of developing and maintaining your own self-awareness, motivation, as well as the new mindsets and behaviours that you'll adopt *for life*.

OVERVIEW AND BENEFITS OF EACH CHAPTER

Chapter One

In chapter one, "Permission to Dream Big," we'll discuss the importance of giving yourself permission to dream big. This will get you started on the path towards realizing those dreams that you never thought were possible to achieve. You'll learn the importance of overcoming distractions and how, without goals, life can become one big distraction. I'll provide insightful analogies that prove how powerful developing a focus can be when you have goals. This will motivate you to stay focused at all costs. In addition, you'll learn the benefits of writing down your goals, and why it is necessary to get the ideas out of your head and on paper. I'll also discuss the importance of taking "baby steps." You'll discover how all success boils down to small steps taken consistently over time. This will enable you to get started on your goals regardless of how big and overwhelming they seem to you. We'll also discuss what goal-setting really means, why it's important, and the many ways that you'll benefit by setting goals for yourself. Knowing this information will help ensure that you never abandon the concept of goals and the important role they will play in your success and satisfaction in life.

Chapter Two

In chapter two, "What Smart Women Know About Goal Setting," you'll learn how to deconstruct traditional rules and myths about goal setting, so that you can understand which rules work best for you and why. Rather than blindly following someone else's rules, you'll discover what the research supports and what some of the blind spots are that misinform women. As a result, you can be confident in your own approach towards achieving your goals and not have to worry or feel guilty that you aren't approaching your goals properly. Finally, I'll introduce a foolproof, fun, and easy-to-use organizational system for your goals that will make it virtually impossible to abandon or forget any of your life goals.

Chapter Three

In chapter three, "The Dreamstorm," you'll benefit by brainstorming a list of all of your important dreams, goals, or ideas of things you'd like to achieve. I have created five categories of goal-setting questions to help stimulate ideas, so that you capture everything that is important to you. We all have many thoughts running through our minds all the time about what we'd like to do with our life, but it's important that we write these ideas down. By completing this first step, you'll be honouring the importance of all your ideas, and capturing them on paper, so they can later be prioritized and evaluated.

Chapter Four

In chapter four, "Prioritize Your Passions," you'll discover how to get more focused than ever before. Have you ever had a list of many different goals, but you were never able to know which ones you should be focusing on? In this chapter, you'll benefit by learning how to clarify which dreams and goals are *the most* powerful and important to you. You'll be able to prioritize your goals by learning how to take different perspectives on what is truly important. By reflecting on the insightful questions that I'll ask you, you'll begin to develop a much clearer idea of where you should be focusing your energies. You'll also learn how, over time, you can work on multiple goals, rather than focusing solely on only one area of your life.

Chapter Five

Chapter five outlines how to write down your most important goals and create plans for achieving them. I'll also discuss the power of visualization and how it can propel you into action more quickly than you ever thought possible. You'll learn how planning can be simplified and streamlined to ensure your success.

Chapter Six

Have you ever found it extremely difficult to stay committed to your goals, despite knowing how important they are to you? In chapter six, I will discuss why achieving our goals and making changes can be very difficult. I'll introduce the research from the scientifically-proven Stages of Change Model and apply this information to goal setting and achievement.

Chapter Seven

In order to obtain commitment to your goals, you will begin by examining your current situation and getting in touch with how you are benefiting from remaining in it. I've developed numerous questions that are fun, creative, and that force you to think about this question from many different perspectives. As a result, your reflection will go to a much deeper level, compared to if I had just asked one straightforward question, "How are you benefitting from your present reality?" The many different insights that you receive will help you understand yourself and your needs much better. Self-awareness is a crucial part in making the necessary changes that are needed to achieve your goals.

Likewise, you'll examine your current situation again. This time, you'll focus on what is negative about it. For example, what are the negative consequences to continuing the way you are presently living? One of the biggest motivators to achieving a goal is getting in touch with just how awful you feel when you are not actually working towards the achievement of your goals. Once again, I've crafted many unique and motivating questions to help you intensify the negativity that you associate with not moving towards your goals.

Chapter Eight

The motivational tasks in this chapter involve examining your potential future and imagining what life will be like when you commit to your goals or achieve your goals. Of course, people have both positive and negative associations to achieving their goals. I'll help you determine what those are. In particular, once you develop a long and *meaningful* list of positive reasons why you should achieve your goals, you'll find yourself instantaneously making some leaps of action towards your goals. The key is to always make sure that your reasons for moving towards your goals are uniquely *your own.* It is not enough to know why you *should* do, be, or achieve something. So, in a nutshell, I'm going to help you discover your own personalized and unique motivation strategies that will set the foundation for turning your compelling desires into unstoppable actions.

Likewise, you'll need to examine some of the negative associations you have towards the goals you want to achieve. Sometimes, people have ambivalent feelings about approaching their goals. On the one hand, they realize all the positive benefits. But, on the other hand, they are paralyzed by some of the negative ideas they have about achieving their goals. This too must be addressed, in order to develop a solid commitment.

As a result of developing a strong commitment to your goals, you will have set the foundation in place that will enable you to easily follow through with your intentions and desires. You'll have done the preparatory work that will make the process of achieving your goals more joyful, easy, and convenient. It will be realistic for you to be able to stick to goals that you have never been able to stick to in the past.

The former steps that I've just talked about are actually the easiest steps. You can develop commitment to your goals and get yourself really psyched up to achieve these goals, but it doesn't mean you'll be that way forever, or even over the long term. For a lot of people, their motivation wanes over time. Is it because they are lazy and not disciplined? Absolutely not! What often becomes a big barrier for many people is changing their limiting belief systems and bad habits. These constantly compete with our motivation and commitment to our goals. You can develop all the motivation in the world, but if you never learn to change your limiting thoughts and attitudes, your efforts towards achieving your goals will be only temporary. Eventually, you'll fall off the wagon.

Chapters Nine to Eleven

In chapters nine, ten, and eleven, you will focus on building a strong foundation for success by identifying and changing both beliefs and behaviours that are holding you back from obtaining success. I will discuss how to identify and challenge your limiting beliefs. Then, I will show you an easy system that will help you "try on" and develop which alternative ways of thinking and believing work best for you. The benefit to you is that you'll be able to remove any feelings of "uncertainty," feeling "blocked," "confused," or the feeling of being limited by your own negative beliefs and attitudes. Wouldn't it be nice to remove the feelings of "uncertainty," "scatteredness," or being blocked, confused, or limited by your own negative beliefs and attitudes? That's what you'll learn to do by reading this book. You'll learn how to create personalized and meaningful mindsets, attitudes, beliefs, thoughts, and feelings that ensure that you follow-through with all the needed actions steps required to achieve your goals.

You will also examine your limiting behaviours—those actions or habits that you engage in that are holding you back. The questions that I'll ask will help you develop customized strategies for discovering new behaviours that you can easily implement in your life. Rather than reading a book where a person is telling you what to do, I'm going to have you brainstorm and problem solve your own behavioural situations, so that the solutions are uniquely your own.

Chapter Twelve

In this chapter, we'll discuss how to keep up your momentum with taking action. You'll learn about the best time-management and motivational tips to ensure that you are unstoppable. We'll also discuss how to deal with barriers that you will run into. On your journey to achieving your many life goals, it is normal and expected to run into barriers or problems. There will be times when your results seem to plateau or you become confused about what is working and what is not. There may be temporary setbacks and roadblocks that leave you puzzled about what to do next. No matter what barriers you are presented with, we'll cover some great problem-solving strategies that will ensure that you can overcome these barriers and move forward on your path to personal achievement.

Chapter Thirteen

The final chapter will close with a few insights that are imperative to hold in your mindset at all times, in order to move forward with your goals. Ready to get started?

CHAPTER 1

Permission to Dream Big!

PERMISSION TO DREAM BIG

> The future belongs to those who believe in the beauty of their dreams.
> -Eleanor Roosevelt

When was the last time you gave yourself permission to sit back and relax with your favourite café latte and to reflect on your life dreams? If you're like most women, it's been way too long. In our culture, we have a set of beliefs, expectations, shoulds, and rules that we often unconsciously adhere to without ever questioning if these beliefs are aligned with who we are. We're taught to go to school, land a steady and high paying job, find the right partner, get married, buy a house, raise children, get a promotion, buy a new car, and then balance career advancement along with promoting the successful development of our children. The list of expectations goes on, and it's different for everyone based on her life context. Societal expectations and norms are a constant for us in our life, and it takes courage to break away from the status quo and question what happiness and success mean to us on a personal level.

I am a firm believer that a big part of being successful and happy begins with allowing ourself to dream big. Dreams are a very exciting way to spark our creativity, and to imagine all of the "what if" scenarios for our life. Dreams are a collection of personal possibilities, fantasies, and visions that we entertain or consider for our future. There are many different ways to entertain or express our dreams: envisioning our dream in vivid detail, creating collages or vision boards, sharing our ideas with other like-minded people, and writing our dreams down on paper. When you give yourself permission to dream big and imagine what kind of success you would like to have, you become closer to removing any personal limits.

You have probably heard from others that dreaming and fantasizing about your future will do you no good, and that what it really takes is action. It is not correct to say that dreaming is a waste of time or that it is silly. Dreaming is not simply wishful thinking. Starting today, I encourage you to give yourself permission to dream big. How are you supposed to achieve your dreams if you have never taken the time to reflect on what they are? Imagining ourself already in possession of our dreams and goals allows us to become immensely excited about our future and to cultivate hope and inspiration.

The truth is, every achievement and goal once started out as a dream. Entertaining our dreams and giving expression to them allow us to imagine what our potential future could be like. It's almost as though we "try on" our dreams for size and comfort before we commit to turning them into goals. The difference between dreams and goals is that dreams are very future-oriented, whereas goals are more concrete, because a person makes a commitment and develops a sense of urgency to achieve the goal. The difference between successful and unsuccessful women is that successful women learn to take their dreams and visions seriously. They don't brush off their dreams as being *only dreams*. Instead, they realize that their thoughts could be things, and the once intangible can turn into something tangible. Only after we have spent time dreaming and thinking big will we be able to set goals, plan, and then act.

Can you remember achieving anything worthwhile that wasn't once a mere thought, idea, or flash of inspiration in the beginning? Realize that no matter how small your accomplishments, they first started out as thoughts and visions that allowed you to become excited and passionate, and that helped motivate you to set goals, take action, and follow through with your needed plans. The process of nurturing our dreams can be compared to the processes that take place in nature. The beautiful trees you see outside started out as tiny seeds in the ground. With regular nurturance from the environment, the seed slowly grew into a huge tree. The whole process does not happen over night, but over a steady and longer period of time. Dreaming is the first step to planting the seeds of success in our mind. Once the seed is planted in our mind, and we give it the needed attention and nourishment, our seed grows into something much bigger, and we can begin to reap the tangible rewards.

I think the key is for women not to set any limits.
-Martina Navratilova

Dreaming big with no limits allows us to think of ideas and possibilities that we *never* thought of before. We become unstoppable with respect to our aspirations. As we dream big, it is as though we stimulate or unlock latent parts of our creative mind. This process is a bit like a snowball effect, because it leads to more and more insights about possibilities for our future. A new sense of self-awareness can be found, and a new space for our future opens up.

IMPORTANCE OF DREAMING BIG

Have you ever planned a vacation? I'm guessing the answer is *yes*. How much time did you spend planning your vacation? My guess is you spent at least several hours. First, you probably spent a good hour casually brainstorming ideas with your family or friends. Then, you might have spent a few hours searching online for hotels to stay at. You might have spent an hour or two driving around the city to pick up maps as well. You probably also made a checklist of things that you would need to pack. By the time you were ready to leave for your trip, you might have easily spent fifteen to twenty hours planning it. How long is the average vacation? I'm guessing one to two weeks. Vacations fly by so quickly. My point is that if you spend so much time planning events, such as your vacations, why wouldn't you do the same with your life? Your life is "forever," but your vacations aren't. What would happen if you gave yourself time and permission to focus on your dreams? Since you will spend hours planning events, such as your dream vacation and wedding, why wouldn't you spend hours planning your other life dreams?

Just don't give up trying to do what you really want to do. Where there is love and inspiration, I don't think you can go wrong.
-Ella Fitzgerald

You might think this is a silly comparison, but making this kind of comparison can give you the leverage needed to focus on your dreams and achieve your goals. How much time have you spent planning other events in your life? Chances are you've probably made a big purchase, such as a home, car, or television. How much time went into thinking and planning for this? But wait. Don't stop there. We can get even crazier about this to really drive the point home. These days, it's easy to spend a good hour planning which laptops, blackberries, or electronic gadgets to buy. I always think about how much time people spend planning and shopping for others' gifts during the holiday season. There are absolutely no excuses for why you cannot create time to reflect on your personal dreams that will have a tremendously positive impact on the rest of your life. Having said that, what prevents us from dreaming big and working towards our goals?

WHAT PREVENTS US FROM DREAMING BIG AND PURSUING OUR GOALS?

Most people live their life in a very distracted way. Simply put, people's lives are often an accumulated product of what they become distracted with in their life. Think about after we arrive home from work after a long day. Our perfect evening includes being able to relax over some tasty food, and then spend a few hours with our children, and then working on one of our personal projects or goals. However, seldom do things ever unfold just as we've planned.

As we walk in the door, the first thing that grabs our attention is the bill sitting on our counter. Knowing that it's almost overdue and that we've been procrastinating for too long, we immediately respond by going online to pay the bill. The online world of course is its own "distraction city." Who doesn't become distracted with interesting articles, or simply getting caught up with emails, Facebook messages, pictures, LinkedIn activity, and the latest YouTube videos? An hour or two of surfing the internet easily goes by in no time. After feeling completely exhausted, you might decide it's time to just soak in a hot tub and unwind. However, as you walk by the kitchen, you realize there are no clean dishes or cutlery, so you can't prepare tonight's dinner or the lunches for the next day, let alone eat something in the morning.

Consumed now by what seems to be a never-ending task, you quickly load the dishwasher and tidy up. Any busy working woman knows that the kitchen alone is perhaps one of the worst distractions at home—perhaps the most distracting of all. Preparing the most basic meals can create many messes and the use of a lot of cutlery. The list of things that can distract us from dreaming big and working on our goals is endless. These are just a few examples of how we all live our daily life in a distracted, busy, or scattered manner. This wouldn't be so bad if it only happened once in a while, but it is problematic when we live on automatic for days, weeks, months, or worse, even years. Without attending to our dreams and goals, it is easy to end up living a life that is less than satisfying.

Each of us has an inner dream that we can unfold if we will just have the courage to admit what it is.
-Julia Cameron

Distractions from our dreams and goals will continue to be present in our life. However, what is more important is how we deal with these distractions. When you have dreams and goals, you still encounter these distractions, but you quickly move past them, *because you know where you are headed—towards your goals*. In other words, being focused is all about maintaining an intentional state of mind and being conscious of how you want to live your life. Of course, this takes time and reflection. You must set aside time to ponder your dreams and what you might want to do, have, or become in your lifetime.

Even then, of course, you can't expect that you'll never be distracted. Distractions are inevitable, normal, and expected. Imagine how much distractions would get the better part of you if you didn't have a clear focus on your life goals. Your situation would be a lot worse.

Another factor that prevents us from pursuing our dreams and goals is that we become overwhelmed with the size of our dreams and with the length of time we assume it will take us to achieve these dreams. We fear that embracing our dreams means a lot of hard work and sweat to make it happen. This is where dreaming big requires us to give ourself further permission to take small steps.

PERMISSION TO TAKE SMALL STEPS

Throughout my journey of personal development, I've realized that great achievements are comprised of a series of small steps, efforts, and actions that evolve over time. It's important that we give ourself permission to take small steps and not become overwhelmed by the size of our dreams or the length of time it might take to achieve them.

Interestingly, we live in a culture in which we are continually bombarded by success stories in the media that misrepresent how people actually achieve their goals. We typically hear about the "rags to riches" stories of people making millions of dollars in the marketplace, or turning a home-based business into a multi-million dollar company, or suddenly becoming a famous actress, and so forth. The media always focus on the end-result of the journey—the destination. No one ever hears about the complex journey that often comes before. This is not to say that huge achievements cannot evolve within a short period of time, because they can and they do. For most people, however, achievement is something that evolves and grows with time.

Sometimes, when we take small steps towards our dreams, we can become confused and misinterpret our action steps as being insignificant. Moving at such a slow and steady pace in a chaotic, fast-paced, results-driven world can be experienced as quite boring, because it doesn't seem like anything is really happening. There are no major outcomes or results that are visible to measure, only your many efforts that you have invested in the process. In fact, you may experience times when you feel as though your efforts lead to nothing. Despite taking consistent action, you might question whether it is all pointless, because you feel as though you are in slow motion and that you are never going to achieve your goals. One reason many people give up dreaming big and pursuing their goals is because achieving their dreams feels almost impossible. As you approach your dreams and begin setting goals, it is wise to exercise patience. Without patience, you may be prone to give up on your dreams altogether.

Start wherever you are and start small.
-Rita Baily

Remember the story of the tortoise and the hare? One day, a hare encountered a tortoise that was slowly moving along an old, beaten path. The hare laughed and mocked the tortoise and bragged about how fast he could run. The tortoise was taken aback, and then decided to challenge the hare for a race. The hare thought it was such a big joke, because there was no way that a tortoise could outpace him. As a result, they both agreed to race. The surrounding animals created a course for the race. When the race began, the swift hare took off with full energy and power, leaving the tortoise far behind. Slowly but surely, the tortoise took many small steps and consistently moved forward. When the hare turned around and couldn't even see the tortoise in sight, he decided to take a little break in a meadow. Because the hare was a little bit tired from going full force, he fell asleep. The tortoise plodded along, step by step, and eventually began approaching the finish line. The animals began to cheer for him, and as a result of the noise, the hare woke up from his nap. Despite trying to catch up to the tortoise, the hare lost the race.

The message behind the story is that slow and steady wins the race. Sometimes, when we push full force towards our goals and go "all out," just like the hare, we are bound to take a break and perhaps tune out from our charted course or forget what our intentions were in the first place. It's always more difficult to get started again after a long pause than it is to take consistent steps forward like the tortoise.

There is a notion in our society that unless we are making leaps and big strides towards our goals, we aren't really getting anywhere. I believe that we all have both the hare and the tortoise tendencies in us. Our hare is like the "yang" energy—that masculine, driving, and often overbearing voice that pushes us to go at full speed with everything in our life. Our tortoise is like the "yin," the feminine energy that, although still intentional, is calm. The reality is that achieving our big goals involves integrating both. It need not constantly be a stressful, exhausting, fast-paced endeavour. If we can overcome this limiting attitude, we are more likely to stretch ourself further with our big goals, because our efforts will be more sustainable over the long run.

Your journey to achieving your dreams is a process as opposed to a single event that happens "overnight."

It's wise to be consistent and develop daily, weekly, and monthly habits that will make your dreams a reality. There is wisdom in knowing when it is time to take leaps and strides versus when it is time to stick to your "baby tortoise steps." Most often, because we are such busy women with other things to attend to, fulfilling our dreams often comes down to our ability to take small steps forward, consistently. Consider how Jill Walser fulfilled her dream by taking small steps forward.

Jill Walser's dream was to run her own career services business, but as a single parent, she couldn't quit her job as a corporate recruiter to start a new business. In 2004, however, she decided to take the first few steps towards embracing her dream. She created a website, obtained a business license, and started assisting clients on evenings and weekends. Her services included resume writing, job search coaching, and interview coaching. Taking these initial steps was important to Jill, because the thought of not being able to pay all her bills when she made the final leap to go independent with her business worried her. She'd be leaving a corporate job with a great salary, benefits, and stock options, and she'd never know when her next client was going to call.

Yet, Jill remained committed to her dream, even though it felt like jumping off a cliff! The insecure and intimidating voice inside her kept saying, *What if your idea doesn't take off? It will be a disaster because you'll have no unemployment benefits.* Rather than remain paralyzed by her fear, she overcame that nagging doubt, and after two years of working on her business in her spare time, she took things one step further. She asked her boss if she could take Wednesdays off to continue building up her business.

Asking for a day off during the week, while working as the company's sole recruiter, felt like a ridiculous request on her part. Each time she asked, she was told that it would be considered, or that she would need to wait until the next manager's meeting, or some other reason that caused a delay. Finally, with much persistence, Jill's request was approved. After originally asking what seemed like an audacious question, it took Jill six months to receive permission to get Wednesdays off. Her boss finally agreed, which was no small feat, considering Jill was the only recruiter for a publicly traded e-commerce company.

Eventually, with this new flexibility, her referral business approached 50 percent (it's now 86 percent) and it no longer made financial sense for Jill to work for someone else. After working four days a week for six months at her corporate job, Jill gave her notice and began operating her own business full time in 2007. Since then, Jill has gone on to offer presentations and workshops in addition to providing writing and coaching services. You can learn more about Jill's services by visiting her website at www.igotthejob.us.

Fulfilling our dreams is about having the courage to take small steps forward. Whether you are taking baby steps, leaps, or great strides with your dreams, remember that the achievement of your dreams is a process that happens gradually and not suddenly.

As busy, savvy women, we need to take comfort in knowing that we are moving forward, period. Sometimes, baby steps are good enough. There really is no race. Instead, we have to learn to set our own pace. My personal motto has always been, "One step a day is the only way."

One step a day is the only way.

Our dreams evolve, because they are nothing more than a series of small steps that evolve into something more, whether it be tangible or intangible. Obtaining success and achieving our dreams is not a one-time event. Rather, it is a process. We can speed up this process by setting goals.

WHAT ARE GOALS?

Our goals are what link our "present behaviour to future outcomes" (King & Burton, 2003). They create discrepancies between our current situation and our desired future states. A goal is nothing more than the "aim of an action" (Latham, 2004). Through goal setting, we enhance our sense of life's meaning and feel more engaged in our life. All behaviour is goal-oriented, even if we don't perceive it that way. "Goal-directed action is an essential aspect of human life" (Latham & Locke, 2006). Everything we do is for some reason, big or small.

The word "goal" is only one piece of language that describes goal-oriented behaviour. That is, there are many different ways to think about what goals are. I sometimes worry that for some women the term has negative connotations. People often think of deadlines, time commitments, and the idea of failure, all of which can prevent them from taking their dreams seriously. So, to help move away from this typical way of thinking about goals, I want to provide several pieces of language, or other ways of thinking about goal setting. The term "goals" has also been used interchangeably with the following:

- Intentions
- Following your passion
- Life projects
- Aims
- Desired changes
- Dreams
- Hopes
- Wishes
- Visions
- Life projects
- Focusing on what is important
- Attending to what you value
- Ambitions
- Fantasies
- Ideas
- Solving meaningful problems for people
- Having a purpose
- Objectives / targets
- Things you want to do, be, or have
- Giving something back

Do any of these words or connotations come to mind when you think about goal setting? If so, then I want you to think about one of these particular words as *your* definition. Goal setting is most effective when you have a way of understanding it, so that it works for you. Substitute these words or ways of thinking in place of the term "goals," as you read this book.

Goal setting is about focusing on whatever is meaningful and important to you.

Think and use whatever language you feel most comfortable with. Interestingly, during the majority of my interviews with successful women, very few of them used the word "goal." Here's a great story to demonstrate this point:

When I interviewed Jaki Scarcello about her goals, she spoke at great length about her personal visions and how she wrote down vision statements to guide her future actions. Her particular vision to help other people led her down an interesting path after she went through a difficult separation with her husband many years before. In search of something more, Jaki went to the library and combed the stacks in hopes of finding a good self-help book. She came across a number of spiritual books by Mouni Sadhu about the Hindu sage Ramana Maharshi. Jaki was inspired by the spiritual messages within these books.

After reading many books and years of working in various roles that supported others in achieving their potential, Jaki became interested in studying aging and peoples' attitudes towards aging. She also became interested in exploring her own spirituality and role as a woman in society. Her journey of achieving her vision unfolded in a series of many small steps.

As a result of asking herself questions, she gained the desire to talk with other women about their experiences. She began by interviewing women in five different countries about their experiences with aging. While Jaki never had the goal to write a book, this process of writing unfolded gradually with one step informing the next. Jaki's writing pursuit was aligned with her life vision, which had in turn developed more specifically to help women learn to age more gracefully and with a sense of spiritual purpose.

In 2005, Jaki remarried. Each year, she joined her author husband on a two-week writing retreat in Spain. During one of these retreats, Jaki spontaneously decided to begin some writing, based on her interviews. As she experimented with her writing, she discovered her unique writer's voice. After the two-week retreat ended, Jaki didn't touch her interviews or writing for an entire year.

The following year, when she and her husband went on another retreat, Jaki decided to continue her writing where she had left off. After this retreat, she again put aside her writing project. Then, six months later, she met a publisher in London. Her husband had scheduled a lunch with the publisher, because he was interested in his friend's books that were published by the company. Jaki was reluctant to mention her own writing project, but thought, *What the heck*, so she told him what she was working on. He was intrigued and requested to read her first chapter. He loved the first chapter so much that he offered to be her publisher! At this point, Jaki was told that she needed a deadline to have the entire book completed. From here, she had to break her writing project down into mini action steps, to be sure the book would be completed on time.

Jaki now has a published book titled, *Fifty and Fabulous! The Best Years of a Woman's Life*. Presently, her focus is to spread the message about fearless aging. Jaki hopes to reach as many women as possible to defy gravity and lift sagging spirits about growing older. She also offers women coaching and delivers workshops to the public. You can learn more about Jaki and her professional services by visiting her website at www.fiftyfab.com

So, just as Jaki preferred to use the word "vision," you, too, may prefer your own language. Don't let the word "goal" throw you off.

WHY IS GOAL SETTING A HOT TOPIC?

Why is goal setting important? Let me answer this question by asking you the opposite question. Why is *not* acting with intention or *not* acting in a goal-oriented manner meaningless?

First, I want to illustrate the importance of setting goals by making comparisons to our everyday behaviour, because all behaviour is goal-oriented. Everything we do is for some reason. We are already setting goals and achieving them as the moments, hours, days, and weeks pass. There is no way to avoid goal setting, really. Although we engage in this behaviour every day, we most often do it in an unconscious way. That is, we aren't aware that we are drawing upon our goal-setting skills.

For me, goals are my road map to the life I want. They have helped me accomplish things I once thought were impossible.
-Catherine Pulsifer

When you bought this book, and now as you are reading it, you have a goal in mind. You are hoping to learn something, or maybe you are simply trying to pass time (hopefully the former!). So, back to the question—why is goal setting important? The importance of goal setting, in part, can be highlighted by understanding that it is an intentional set of skills that we are already using every day. We use it for daily satisfactions or for behaviours that other people expect of us. What would happen if we started applying this set of goal-setting skills to our future? What if we decided to act so intentionally on our future desires and plans?

If our goal-oriented behaviour works so well in our day-to-day activities, why not apply what we know about it to our big goals? I can tell you why people aren't accustomed to doing this. Many people are overwhelmed by the phrase "goal-setting." Why? Because it seems to imply something significant or a big achievement. Setting goals and achieving them has a connotation that there is something we want, but that it is out of our reach. We also fear being too busy, tied up, and worst of all, risking failure.

This is why I believe people don't set goals, especially goals for the long term. It is overwhelming and not convenient to think about the future. However, I want you to realize the importance and benefits of goal setting, and why it is a necessary set of skills you should consider developing more consciously.

THE AMAZING BENEFITS OF GOAL SETTING

We have always been told to set goals if we want to be high achievers. In fact, I'll bet many people even take this advice for granted. After all, we hear it so much that we don't know what to do with it.

If you want to start setting goals, but you are having difficulty getting motivated, then you need to understand the reasons for goal setting. Without knowing the benefits of setting a goal, you are unlikely to engage in any efforts or actions past the "dreaming" stage.

1. Developing a Clear Focus

One key benefit of goal setting is that it gives you a clear, specific focus to attend to the necessary action steps needed to achieve your goal (Latham & Locke, 2006). Think about all the important accomplishments that you achieved in your past. How did you achieve them? I'm guessing that any important accomplishment first involved identifying and getting specific about what it was that you wanted in the first place. You cannot take action steps towards any goal without first having a goal.

> *Ask for what you want and be prepared to get it.*
> *-Maya Angelou*

Here's how and why this works. There is something in our brain called a reticular activating system. Every time we write down a goal that we want to achieve, our reticular activating system creates an impression of this goal in our mind (Canfield, 2005). Our brain then does everything in its power to help us pay attention to information, resources, solutions, ideas, opportunities, and people who can help us achieve this goal. As a result, we are much more focused on achieving our desired outcomes (Latham & Locke, 2006).

This is also common sense. Think back to the last time you identified and then bought a new style of clothing or jewellry. After your purchase, did you suddenly notice that many other women seemed to be wearing the same piece of jewellry or clothing style that you had just bought? This is your reticular activating system hard at work, trying to draw your attention towards your own goal. When you write down your goals, your brain focuses your attention on your goals more seriously.

2. A Sense of Control and Autonomy

Another great benefit of goal setting is that when you are actively writing down goals and planning out your future, it gives you a sense of control and autonomy. It is a way of demonstrating your commitment to achieving your goal. You are literally programming your brain and putting in an order to increase your chances of your goal becoming a reality. So, how can you not feel in control of your life when you set goals?

Goal setting is also a strategy for setting standards for how to live your life. None of us needs to settle, because we all deserve to experience "the best" that life offers. This will be different for each of us. Once you set standards for your life, you'll be less likely to engage in activities that aren't compatible with your authentic self and goals. Without clear standards, you might be prone to becoming more distracted and settling for whatever comes your way.

3. High Self-esteem

When you feel in control of your life, your self-esteem is also likely to increase. How can you *not* feel good about yourself when you are in the "driver's seat" of your own life, turning your dreams into reality? As a result of feeling great about yourself, you'll begin to create a lot of momentum with your life goals. Like a snowball getting larger and larger, you'll begin to accumulate more and more accomplishments in the different areas of your life. This in turn creates a lot of unstoppable energy and leverage for you to begin taking all sorts of new actions.

4. Passion for Life

Overall, you will feel a greater sense of passion, excitement, and personal engagement in your life. Goal setting has been found to energize people (Latham, 2004). As you set and write down your goals, it should make you feel thrilled that you are beginning a new commitment to what is important to you.

Passion is energy. Feel the power that comes from focusing on what excites you.
-Oprah Winfrey

You might have heard the saying, "Half of success is simply showing up." This reminds me of my personal advice to you: Half of success is getting clear on what your goals are and writing them down. I know in my own experience, simply identifying my goals gave me a lot of passion, zest, and confidence, which in turn led to further momentum.

5. Improved Psychological and Physical Well-being

Setting goals and working towards their achievement increase our subjective well-being or how we feel psychologically along with also improving our physical well-being. We experience decreased levels of depression and increased levels of positive emotions when we feel that we are succeeding with the achievement of our goals (King & Burton, 2003). In addition, we experience increased levels of happiness, joy, and satisfaction with our life (Latham & Locke, 2006).

6. Life Purpose and Meaning

Setting and pursuing the accomplishment of goals provide us with a sense of meaning and life purpose (Locke & Latham, 1984), as opposed to randomly going with the flow and simply reacting to the external stimuli in our life. It would also make sense that meaningful goal setting relieves us of our boredom (Latham, 2004) and the daily monotony of other routines.

If you are smart, you will try to remember all the benefits you will reap if you set goals, because the more positive reasons you have for doing something, the more likely you are to do it.

7. Increased Learning and Development

Naturally, as we set out to achieve our goals, we can't help but stretch who we are as a person. We grow and evolve, as we take on new challenges and pursuits. At the same time, we are forced to learn new strategies to solve problems, overcome roadblocks, and stay motivated. We expand who we are by doing things we've never done before. As a result of our continual learning and nurturing of our brains, we keep them "younger" as opposed to "older" and we increase our brain's capacity for further learning and development with respect to achieving our goals.

8. Productivity

When we set out to achieve a goal, we are forced to become more productive, efficient, and organized. This has been referred to as the "Hawthorne Effect" (Locke & Latham, 1984) in which our focused attention automatically makes us more productive. Our self-management skills improve as well as our overall performance in life. This also means that we accomplish our goals much more quickly than if we hadn't set goals. We also begin to accumulate more and more practical achievements (Latham, 2004). It's no wonder that we also become more persistent (Latham & Locke, 2006) and motivated in our goal pursuits.

Okay, so now that we've discussed the benefits of goal setting, how are we supposed to set our goals? What do smart women know about this process?

CHAPTER 2

What Smart Women Know About Goal Setting

IS THE "SMART" WAY THE RIGHT WAY?

> Sometimes questions are more important than answers.
> -Nancy Willard

When was the last time you heard about the SMART way to set goals and as a result became extremely frustrated with its trite and seemingly superficial principles? Have you ever wondered if this popular acronym is even valid, and if it is the best way for women to set goals? The acronym states that when setting our goals, they are supposed to be very Specific, Measurable, Attainable with a detailed plan, Realistic, and Time-bound (must have a deadline).

I recently came across Schachter's (2010) article in the *Report on Business* in which the first sentence of the article read, "SMART goals are dumb." I was relieved to learn that others were catching onto the fact that, while the SMART acronym does have substance, it is not an all-encompassing approach to goal setting at all. The truth is that none of my achievements has resulted from abiding by this formula, and none of the women I interviewed for this book attributed their success to this formula, either.

When it comes to your own success, it's important to question common rules and assumptions about the right way to achieve something. The SMART formula has become a bit trite, and sometimes, the rationales behind it don't make a lot of sense. For example, I laugh when I hear people raise the question, "How will you know if you've achieved your goals unless they are measurable?" I think if you had a big enough goal, you would know without a doubt when it was achieved. Otherwise, you might want to consider setting a more ambitious goal for yourself. I'm *not* dismissing the value and wisdom of the SMART formula. I will share with you what the actual research indicates about many of the key concepts inherent in the SMART formula. The more research I conducted, the more I realized the SMART formula couldn't be interpreted as an all-encompassing theory. The SMART formula has its flaws and seems to only address half of the "success equation," when it comes to achieving big goals.

As a smart and savvy woman, you deserve to know what works and what doesn't. In working with many women over the years, I've both observed and always had the hunch that women's ways of knowing and their approach to achieving their life dreams and goals differ from what is taught in the widespread and popular SMART acronym. As a result, I decided to interview women on their success stories to learn about the role that goal setting played in their journey. I was not surprised that *none* of the women had attributed their success with achieving their goals to the SMART formula.

SMART goal setting has many valuable benefits that should not be ignored, so I wouldn't advocate that you throw the baby out with the bath water. However, SMART goal setting seems to only speak to the logical, mechanistic, and "scientific" side of the "success" equation, leaving out other subjective, important variables, such as a person's life context and personal preferences. I believe it has also turned many women off from the practice of goal setting. When I think about this formula on its own, there are certain negative connotations and overlooked concerns that immediately come to mind.

We often start off with vague dreams or goals. With further time and attention, they crystallize into something more specific.

WHAT'S SPECIFIC GOT TO DO WITH IT?

Let's start with the first guideline of setting a specific goal. Being specific with your goals is very important, however, "specific" on its own leaves out an important former step—the need for exploration, reflection, curiosity, and something else that we refer to as dreaming or thinking big. This is how the process of goal setting should begin. But if one focuses only on the SMART acronym, this process of dreaming big is overlooked. Setting a specific goal first begins with considering the bigger picture of your life and what is important to you.

The first time you actually get serious and start thinking about what you want in your life, you will come up with many different ideas, and this is exactly what you need to do. The term "specific" on its own can be limiting in nature. How does one have absolute clarity and detail on a goal that is in its infancy?

The truth is, the clarity of your goals will evolve and develop over time. When I interviewed women on their experiences with achieving their life goals, the majority of them did *not* have such specific goals to start with. Instead, they spoke of visions, dreams, and general intentions—all of which over time were refined into more specific goals. In fact, many of the women spoke about their goals almost as an after effect of their dreams maturing, crystallizing, or coming to fruition. It's as if there is a natural development process in which, when we nurture our dreams, they ripen into something more definite or tangible which makes it easier to set a specific or concrete goal.

So, don't worry if the visions behind your goals in the different areas of your life are a bit vague in the beginning. This is completely normal when you are first setting goals. Instead of thinking about getting specific with details, think about finding a general aim that you will move closer to with time. In other words, when you first start writing down your goals, they might be quite general. Eventually, with time, the more often you write, think about, and talk to others about your goals, the more clear they will become.

The reason I am often turned off by "specific" as being a way to set one's goals from the outset is because it can shut down or limit people's creativity and curiosity right from the beginning. The reality is that, in the beginning and quite possibly even for weeks or months, your goal might be akin to a little seed that needs lots of nurturance and development. Being specific with your goals certainly does have its place. However, it is a matter of eventually refining them in time, when you are clearer on your intentions.

BENEFITS OF SPECIFIC GOALS

Your "goal" is unlikely to be specific in the beginning and that is why I often refer to it as a "dream." Each time you revisit your dreams or goals, you'll want to do your best to describe them in as much detail as possible. The benefit to gaining further clarity around your goal is that you will experience more motivation and momentum, because you'll find it easier to know which resources, people, and action steps are the most suited to you and your unique situation. If your goal is the type of goal that you want to "measure," then obviously, the more detailed your goal is, the easier it will be to measure. We'll discuss this more later.

Some studies have demonstrated that specific goals are more likely to be achieved than non-specific goals (also known as "do my best" goals), because a person will put forth more effort when there is a clear benchmark of achievement by which to evaluate one's progress (Locke & Latham, 2002). There is also some common sense to why people might choose to get specific with their goals.

Consider a person who is working as a full-time employee, but is completely unsatisfied with her job, and wants a new job. It's great that she knows that she wants a new job, but what if she's unsure of what type of job she is looking for? Without having developed some degree of clarity around the goal, it will be difficult for her to navigate through all the opportunities that she encounters. She may become overwhelmed, discouraged, and feel quite scattered. There is also less urgency, because she doesn't feel pulled towards any one type of opportunity specifically. Eventually, however, she might get so sick and tired of her job, that she decides to make a hasty, ill-informed decision and take up a friend on a job offer. With no real knowledge of what she was really looking for in the first place, chances are great that she is only stepping into another rut that is similar to the one she was already in, all because she couldn't identify what she wanted.

You can't achieve your dreams unless you know what those dreams are!

I'm now going to reiterate the point, because it is so important. How will you ever achieve your dreams if you don't know what they are? This is why it's so important to take time to brainstorm and reflect on all the dreams within you. If you don't ever put them on paper to explore them, you may not get the eventual clarity that you're looking for. We'll do a "dreamstorm" session of your dreams in chapter three. Because achievement is so important to you, you must eventually define what it is that you want. The first step to doing this is to give yourself permission to dream big!

Once you gain clarity on your dreams, you'll naturally develop more and more specific goals. It will become easier for you to pay attention and recognize the great opportunities, people, and resources that come your way. For example, let's say that you know one of your goals involves the desire to write. It's a little bit like peeling back the layers of an onion. In time, as you peel off the layers, you gain further clarity and decide that you want to write an actual book. Then, you realize that you have a desire to write fiction. Lastly, you discover that you want to write a romantic fiction book, and you want it to become a best seller. As a result of having developed this clarity, you'll begin to easily recognize opportunities that will help you pursue your goal. You might notice advertisements on how to write fiction, whereas in the past you wouldn't notice them at all, because they weren't relevant or of immediate need at the time. You might actually pay attention to the ads in the magazines that promote a course titled, *How to Write a Best Selling Romance Novel.* Had you not known you wanted to pursue this specific goal, these opportunities would not have stood out so loud and clear for you.

Specific goals allow you to focus your energy, time, and resources on what you want, enabling you to achieve your goals.

Another great example is having the goal to purchase a new house. On its own, it is a very general goal. Once it becomes more specific, e.g., a two-story, yellow brick house, with hardwood floors, walk-in closets, and skylights, then it becomes much easier for the buyer and realtor to find the "perfect" house.

This concept is so obvious, but few people apply this principle holistically to all their life goals. What would happen if you had the courage to stand by your dreams and allow yourself to get really specific on what you wanted? The message is that over time, you do want to gain more clarity around your goals. Otherwise, you won't notice the many different opportunities, resources, and people that are necessary for you to tap into, in order to achieve your goals.

Remember, however, in the beginning, as you explore your dreams, it is perfectly natural to *not* know the specifics, and this is completely normal. Your aim is to commit to your dreams, and over time your goals will become more specific.

THE DANGERS OF BEING TOO SPECIFIC

There is a lot of value in being specific with your goals, but being too specific and developing a narrow focus can also turn things sour if you are not cautious (Kayes, 2005). Many examples of how specific goals can be limiting have been noted within organizational contexts (Ordonez, Schweitzer, Galinksy, & Bazerman, 2009), and the same principle holds true for individuals pursuing their goals. For example, sometimes, we can get so excited and focused on a goal that our narrow focus causes us to unconsciously neglect other parts of our life in which we haven't set goals. We might set really important career goals and be completely passionate about them, however, we may actually do damage to our relationships by not spending time with the people who are important to us. I have heard numerous stories from my clients throughout the years, who had invested so much time, energy, and effort into a project at work, only to later discover that their marriage was on shaky ground.

I also counselled a woman who became so involved in starting her own business that she literally worked fifteen-hour days. Of course, she loved the work so much that she didn't consider it a problem. Her myopic focus and abundance of energy seemed like such a great asset on the surface. However, she ended up gaining forty pounds in one year from excessive eating. She was experiencing what is called "euphoric stress"—the type of stress, anxiety, and "hyperness" that results from positive life events. The effect of the stress is overlooked, because it is experienced in the context of positive things happening that distract one from the negative effects. In this case, this woman literally became over-identified with her goal so much that she no longer cooked, bought groceries, or exercised. She gave it all up for this one goal. The tragedy was that her health soon caught up with her so much that she had a heart attack in her early fifties. While specific goals are important, we must make sure they don't limit or prevent us from attending to the other areas of our life that are just as important. This is yet another reason why it makes sense to have goals in *all* areas of your life, so as to create a state of balance.

Being too specific or set on one particular goal, approach to a goal, or a particular life path can cause you to miss out on other opportunities or approaches that might be even more beneficial to you than your original plan. This has been referred to as "planned happenstance" (Mitchell, Levin, & Krumboltz, 1999). It stresses the importance of being open to new opportunities that differ from your original plans or goals. While we must focus on our specific goals and plans, we must still remain open-minded and curious about potential alternative opportunities, paths, resources, and ideas for how we can achieve our life dreams.

WHAT'S THE BIG HYPE WITH MEASUREMENT?

There is a lot of merit behind the concept of measurement. It is actually a very powerful principle. Like anything, it has its downfalls, of course. I've observed that many individuals associate the principle of measurement only with the final outcome of their goals, as opposed to incremental progress. The potential problem is that the final "outcome" or the achievement of a person's goal might take many weeks, months, or even years to attain. People can become so focused on the end achievement of their goals that they forget to measure the progress made throughout their journey. I believe that we need to measure and reward ourself for the many steps, actions, and efforts along the way, even if it hasn't led to the final outcome. Doing so provides us with positive reinforcement, a source of motivation that will inspire us to keep taking action towards our goals.

I recommend always measuring and tracking your efforts. For instance, what do you know now that you didn't know beforehand with respect to one of your goals? As a result of your efforts, what is different now? What have you tried up until now and what have you learned as a result? Working towards the achievement of our goals is not always a linear process that generates tangible results for each effort put forth. As a result, it's wise to be creative in our approach to measurement. Rather than thinking only in terms of "measurement" and numbers, try thinking also in terms of "tracking" your efforts and corresponding learning lessons.

There do seem to be some goals that aren't as conducive to being measured by quantifiable standards. For instance, what if a person's goal is to maintain a positive outlook on life? What if a person's goal is to experience more gratitude on a daily basis? Not everyone wants to "translate" or break those goals into something quantifiable. Not everyone wants to take a "logical" approach to every single goal.

On the flip side, of course, there are many short-term, straightforward goals that are easy to measure, such as the size of your waist, your bank account, or perhaps the number of unique visitors that arrive at your website each month. These types of goals are easy and fun to measure, because they are quite concrete. However, not all goals are so straightforward. Therefore, it is useful to get into the habit of also tracking your efforts and lessons learned.

ATTAINABLE AND ACTION-ORIENTED

We are taught to make sure our goals are attainable. In other words, can they be achieved? Part of answering this question involves asking yourself if you can act on your goals or take action towards them. Of course, this is important. It's a no brainer. Our goals must be broken down into action steps. Did you know that taking action is *not* most people's weakness? It's relatively easy to take action. Consider the common New Year's resolution to lose weight. People get into action right away, but they often have problems *staying* in action.

The downside to promoting the "massive action" side of the equation is that it leaves out an equally important task—planning, especially for roadblocks and lack of motivation. Many people in life know what to do to achieve their goals. The problem they often have is sticking to their goals or *following through* with their goals. In fact, the missing link in the research on goal setting and resolutions is understanding a person's motivation to stick with it (Koestner, 2008). We'll be addressing this later.

In order to do goal setting and make the necessary changes involved in success, a person needs to work on identifying her limiting beliefs or thoughts and behaviours, and supplementing them with new ones (Prochaska, Norcross, & Diclemente, 1994). This requires work. Compared to taking action, it is relatively boring for most people, as it is the "behind the scenes" work, and not something that you can easily measure and track. Luckily, this is something I'm going to assist you with in this book, so that nothing holds you back from moving closer towards your goals.

Another way to think about the importance of taking action is to constantly be in the habit of moving towards your goals by taking small baby steps. You don't have to rush out and try to accomplish everything tomorrow. Slow it down and focus on making smaller strides at a slow and steady pace. Aside from not overwhelming yourself, another advantage to this approach is that when you run into what seems like a big roadblock, you will take the same approach to solving this problem. You'll take baby steps to try to navigate through the problem, rather than letting it paralyze and stop you altogether. So, give it a shot and break your big goals down into small action steps that you can easily attain.

CAN A DREAMER REALLY BE REALISTIC?

The SMART formula teaches us that our goals should be realistic. When you are first setting goals, the last thing I'd recommend is to be realistic. This assumption again is rooted in thinking out of practicality and logic. What about thinking big? For instance, consider Jack Canfield and Mark Victor Hansen's goal to turn their idea for the *Chicken Soup for the Soul* books into a best seller that would sell one and a half million copies. Does that sound realistic? Hardly.

When you're first starting to get in touch with your dreams and big goals, thinking realistically will counteract your efforts.

The first step is to decide on what you want in the different areas of your life, and only later to figure out the "how." The "how" is your plan, and this is the component that will be rooted in practicality. Your idea itself can be "big," but your plan to get there must be realistic. Don't ever let your current lack of awareness or knowledge prevent you from attempting to achieve a dream of your choice. I once read that being realistic with setting your goals is actually being pessimistic. So, think big, and don't consider realistic plans in the beginning. That part of your plan and strategy will come later. So, think big, set high standards, and be courageous with your goals. Do not limit yourself. This is your chance to design your life, so adopt a lofty mindset! If you don't achieve your big goal, at least you increase your chances of achieving more as opposed to less.

Here's why we should think about having big goals. Some research shows that, in general, **the more difficult our goal is, the better are our chances of reaching the goal.** This idea has been demonstrated over and over again in sports achievement (Weinburg, Harmison, Rosenkranz, & Hookom, 2005). It has also been noted for both organizational and individual performance (Latham & Locke, 2007). As long as a person has the necessary knowledge, resources, and commitment to her goal, and provided she doesn't have conflicting goals, there is a direct, positive relationship between a tough goal and the effort that she puts forth. In terms of our goal achievement, there are few limits except our own mind. Since it takes the same amount of time, energy and, effort to set a "big" or "difficult" goal versus a "small" or "easy" goal, why not go big?

If you're going to spend time and energy thinking about your goals, why wouldn't you think big?

Other research has shown that individuals are more motivated and perform better when their goals are of moderate difficulty (Locke & Latham, 1990) as opposed to too easy or too difficult. Don't misperceive this as meaning that you should be *realistic* with your goals. The best way to interpret this research is that being realistic is about taking small action steps, so we can gain momentum. It means that your *short-term goals* or the action steps themselves need to be of moderate difficulty, i.e., not too easy and not too hard. This is common sense, because we need some positive reinforcement in the short term to feel good about what we're achieving. Short-term or "realistic" action steps help us accomplish this. But with respect to the big picture and the final outcome, don't ever limit yourself. Believe in your dreams and think big! The higher you set the bar, the more you'll accomplish in the long term.

COMPLETE YOUR GOAL BY THE DEADLINE, *OR ELSE WHAT?*

Last, but not least, watch out for the time-bound notion of the *deadline*. My goodness, what feelings and thoughts come to mind when you hear the term "deadline"? The term seems to imply that you ought to achieve your goal by a certain date *or else*. Automatically, many people may feel a lot of negative pressure and stress.

It almost feels like a competition to "beat the clock," so to speak. There is a feeling of needing to rush and possibly sacrifice quality to meet the deadline. There is also the fear of failure. If you don't achieve your goal by the deadline, you might feel like a failure. This can create feelings of low self-worth and unnecessary frustration and stress (Latham & Locke, 2006). Worry and anxiety are common side effects of goal-setting (King & Burton, 2003), and are likely in great part due to the pressure of meeting a deadline.

Deadlines, of course, are important, and they will have a necessary time and place with many of your goals. When the tasks are quite basic and straightforward, it makes sense to set a date for their completion, because achieving the goal doesn't require any complex problems to solve (Latham & Locke, 2006). The pursuit of many other life goals however, aren't so straightforward. The achievement of big goals and dreams are rather complex. Rather than focusing exclusively on an end-result or destination, many dreams are likely to unfold one step at a time. Our achievements evolve, and it is a journey-oriented process.

The key isn't so much to focus on the quantity of time it takes to achieve our goals. Rather, it's about the commitment to our goals. It's about staying focused and knowing the direction we are headed in. If there is a single benefit of having a deadline, it's that it forces us to increase our focus on taking actions to complete our goals. When we are pressed for time, we must use our time accordingly. However, when our goals are quite complex, we can't always control timelines, due to the unexpected variables that always come into play during our journey. For instance, deadlines assume that one already has all the resources in place, and that one already knows the exact instructions on how to arrive at the goal. It also assumes a person will have no obstacles or barriers to overcome, which in turn, takes time to circumnavigate.

The problem is that for savvy women like us, who have big dreams, they can't be achieved by following a cookie-cutter approach. We can't reduce our goals to a socially-constructed "formula." There is no precise instruction manual with a person's name carved into it. A person's unique circumstances always come into play, and rarely are there any detours.

Rather than thinking in terms of deadlines, it makes better sense to think about moving or "evolving" targets. The achievement of our goals is a dynamic process that is constantly in flux. Changes in our environment, available resources, and the unique factor of "trial and error" all ensure unexpected zig zags in our path, and hence our overall timeline.

As a person works towards achieving her goals, she is constantly customizing her plans and overall approach. As time goes on, we constantly evaluate our goals, their importance, relevance, and meaning to us.

Another assumption inherent in deadlines is that a person will always be consistent in her motivation to plan, take action, and adjust her approach as needed. This is rarely the case, because what gets a person from Point A to Point B is always different than what is required to move a person from Point B to Point C. New plans and new perspectives and meanings for staying motivated are always required.

The reality is that most people don't know how to stay motivated all the time or even *most* of the time. I've realized that learning personal motivation techniques is perhaps even more difficult than taking action, because motivation is what gets a person to take action, and *to take action consistently*.

Have you ever wondered why you often hear the advice to attach a deadline to your goal? Part of it comes down to Parkinson's Law, which states that your efforts and time invested in a goal will increase in proportion to the amount of time you give yourself. According to this theory, it is assumed that whether a person gives herself a month or a year, it will require a similar amount of time to fulfill her goal. The reason is that if the deadline is tighter, we'll work faster and harder or find other ways to finish more quickly. This is why in the workplace you probably experience tight deadlines from your supervisors. The deadlines also create a certain degree of pressure and motivation.

For some people, deadlines motivate them, and for others, it can make them so anxious they won't take any action at all. In my opinion, there are some types of goals for which it makes sense to work within a deadline. Research shows that when the tasks and amount of increased effort behind a goal are easy and straightforward, and require little to no complex problem solving, then it's great to have a tough goal along with a deadline. However, as soon as novel or complex tasks or goals are introduced into the equation, the value of a tight deadline may be dubious (Latham & Locke, 2006). For example, a goal to clean the house, or to complete filing in the office, or to complete a list of basic errands would be well suited to a tight deadline perhaps. However, if the goal is complex and requires a lot of problem solving and if the person is exploring new terrains, the deadline might not be as practical, but might instill a lot of guilt.

Goal setting is most successful when the amount of a person's effort invested in her goal directly and positively impacts her goal's progress. However, when pursuing a complex goal for the first time, in which a lot of learning is involved, and in which there could be many possible approaches to tackling the goal, goal setting may have a less than favourable effect. Goal setting is most appropriate when a person is concerned with the quantity of their output rather than the quality. When challenged with a new task that is complex, one might be wise to try their best instead of striving for an exact outcome or goal (Kayes, 2006). Goals that focus on learning as opposed to strict performance are most recommended for goals that seem very complex, complicated, and overwhelming due to their intricate nature.

Whether or not you use deadlines is a personal preference. Know yourself and your work style. If you're going to use a deadline, make it realistic (Locke & Latham, 2006). Otherwise, it might be best to position your goals as an evolving process.

POSITION YOUR GOALS AS AN EVOLVING PROCESS

Achieving our goals is not a single event. Rather, it is an evolving process. Our achievements evolve, one step at a time, one day at a time, one insight at a time, and this occurs over and over again. The journey is forever evolving. The notion of a deadline implies that the journey ends once the destination is arrived at. However, the journey continues as a person maintains, improves, or builds upon that big dream. A deadline is also associated with a "cut-off point," after which point a person might subconsciously assume that she should not even bother pursuing her goals any further. Also, what happens when you keep on missing your deadline? This is something the SMART formula doesn't address. An inherent risk in setting tight deadlines and then not meeting them is that a person could experience a sense of failure (King & Burton, 2003).

Taking small, continual steps creates the building blocks on which we achieve our big goals.

Being "smart" about achieving your dreams isn't only logical, it also requires being present to your own unique life context. Rather than relying exclusively on someone else's cookie-cutter formula, you might want to take a few of the main principle ingredients that are compatible with your personality and work style, and create your own personalized recipe for success. Others' expertise and advice combined with your own self-knowledge and inevitable trial and error might prove to be the most fruitful.

It is not just about staying fully committed to a set of predetermined and specific goals with dates attached to them, it also requires being open and receptive to the many new opportunities, perspectives, and learning lessons that develop as each day passes. We are in constant flux and change. Therefore, our goals must reflect this as well.

Goal setting is about living with passion and staying focused on your multiple, evolving dreams. The SMART approach to setting goals is one of two important sides of the equation. Use your imagination, intuition, and personal wisdom to adopt an approach that works for you. In the end, there is no one exact acronym, formula, or secret that can get you there. What works for someone else might not work for you.

WHAT IF I DON'T FOLLOW THE RULES?

Don't worry if you don't write your goals down exactly as my or other peoples' instructions suggest. It has been proposed that *the way* you write down your goal may not be enough to guarantee success (Koestner, 2008). For this reason, I'm not devoting much emphasis to this topic. The challenges of following something, such as the SMART formula and how you write down your goals are trivial compared to what comes after you've written down your goals. What might be even more important for predicting your success is your ability to plan, motivate yourself, and follow through in the face of adversity. For these reasons, I've only given you a few suggestions on the technical piece of how you write down your goals. There are many different sets of instructions for how you should write down your goals. However, what you do or don't do after you write down your goals is much more important.

WRITE YOUR DREAMS AND GOALS DOWN ON PAPER!

Let me share with you a personal experience that convinced me of the power of writing goals down. What's interesting is that I didn't follow a specific formula as above, or the SMART formula which you read everywhere. Although extensive research has demonstrated the power of writing down your goals in a methodical manner, it seems as though different strategies work for different people.

Going back to the days when I was studying for my undergraduate degree, I remember going through a period of time in which school became *really* boring for me. I would sit in the library between my classes. I remember not doing homework, but instead, wanting to escape the mental dryness of my day-to-day activities. I'm not sure how the process started exactly, but I remember writing my dreams down on paper.

In retrospect, my initial writing was more like doodling. I was enjoying the process of expressing my aspirations on paper in a very idealistic sense. Sometimes, my writing took the form of jotting points down, and sometimes, I was more elaborate, using sentences. Organization and flow of my thoughts did not matter. Rather, it was setting an intention for myself. What was most important was the expression of my aspirations and writing them down.

As I did this, I remember immediately feeling a sense of utopia and great calmness, as if I were living in a fantasy. I also began to feel guilt, as if I were just wasting time. But whatever I was doing felt too good to stop. Even though, at first, it seemed like a silly and unproductive act, I continued to write each day about my goals as a way to explore this enormous amount of excitement and tension that was building up inside me. Soon, I was writing for at least an hour each day. I never thought of this as goal setting *per se*. I just considered it to be a bit of a self-indulgent, enjoyable process. However, through my writing, I began to feel swirls of creative, ambitious, and intentional energy. So, I continued to write my aspirations and goals down every single day.

It seemed as though what was happening was an attempt to rapidly organize and design my life on paper. Not only was I excited about recording my dreams and goals, but through my writing, I began to realize that I had a burning desire to share this information with other people. A theme that began to evolve out of writing down my goals was that I wanted to try motivational speaking.

Despite my excitement, I had a limiting belief that I could not do this, because I had never experienced any major life achievements or hardships. However, as I kept writing, I experienced a sense of conviction that my passion for personal growth and goal setting was enough justification for me to speak to other people regarding these topics. Staying with my ideas and nurturing them consistently through my writing somehow transformed how serious I was about my goals. They began to feel so real, as if I was already experiencing ahead of time what it would be like to execute my goals. I felt very close to my ideas and developed a profound sense of trust and urgency that I should move forward and begin the process of taking action. Within a matter of weeks, I surprised myself with something extraordinary. Because my desire was so strong, I actually quit my job, and within a matter of days, I was on the phone contacting social organizations and elementary schools, asking them if they'd like to have a guest speaker for a goal-setting workshop.

Within a short amount of time, I began creating these workshops and spent several months presenting them to the community. I am still taken aback at how powerful the process of writing down my aspirations was. Although I didn't use an exact formula, I believe that what propelled me into action was my inner sense of clarity and conviction that I would turn my desire into a reality. The more I wrote down this aspiration, the more motivation and confidence I had within me. The reason I've shared this story with you is because I don't think any of this would have been possible unless I had given myself time and permission to reflect upon my aspirations and ideas for what was important to me. So, ask yourself: Are you willing to give yourself permission to take part in this process? What have you got to lose?

> *Life is either a daring adventure or nothing at all.*
> *Security is mostly a superstition. It does not exist in nature.*
> *—Helen Keller*

BENEFITS OF WRITING DOWN YOUR GOALS

Writing down your goals is similar to writing a code to execute a computer program. Without the code, the computer has no instructions and will not operate. Your mind really isn't any different. When you write down your goals, you are creating a personalized "success blueprint." Each goal that you write down provides your mind with a "code" that programs your mind to take action towards these goals. Why is it so beneficial to write our goals down on paper? While there are literally many benefits to writing down your goals, I'll hone in on the six key benefits.

1. Turning the Intangible into Something Tangible

Writing your goals down is the first step to turning them into something real and concrete. Writing them down is about giving yourself the permission, the "okay," to go ahead and start making these goals a reality. It's about setting things into motion and formalizing a commitment to your goals. Your dreams begin to move from something intangible to tangible, from imaginary to real. Turning thoughts and wishes into written words that you can actually see and read moves your goals one step closer to being achieved. Holding a dream in your head demonstrates interest, whereas writing your dream on paper means that you are much more serious. It's similar to how contracts are used in the business world. However, you are demonstrating a formality, through a personal written contract, that you are committed to achieving your personal goals. It is not enough to think about your goals and only keep them in your mind. When your goals are only in your mind, they exist in an indefinite, vague form. At this point, they are only dreams and wishes. When you write your goals down, however, you're conveying to yourself and the world that you mean business.

2. Visualization

Another benefit has to do with the power of the written language and corresponding visualization. When you use written language to express your goals, you can't help but visualize the corresponding pictures of your goals that come into your mind.

These images create an experiential process that stirs up many positive emotions around your goal. What ends up happening is that you begin to experience your goals as if they were already happening right now, in the present. You create a state of mind in which you feel as if you are already in the process of achieving these goals, and indeed, by writing the goals down, you *are* in the process of making your goals happen.

3. Discover Opportunities

The process of identifying and writing down your goals programs your reticular activating system, which is a component of your brain that keeps you alert to paying attention to people, resources, and opportunities that will help you achieve your goals. In fact, it can make the process of achieving your goals seem almost automatic. Do you remember the last time you decided what new car to purchase? After you identified the new car, you probably began to notice that car everywhere you went. You automatically noticed it, because your reticular activating system had flagged it as an important goal.

4. Quit Forgetting About Your Goals!

Capturing your goals on paper will prevent you from forgetting about them. As silly as it sounds, I believe many people over time do forget about their goals, because we all have busy lives and are constantly distracted by something called life. When you record your goals on paper, you are imprinting them to memory. Even if you go through a period of time when you are quite busy, you can always return to your notebook or journal and quickly refresh and refocus on your goals again.

5. Lifelong Clarification and Prioritization of Goals

Finally, another important note about capturing your goals on paper is that over time, you will discover which ones are truly important to you. Your goals which are first expressed as ideas, thoughts, and desires, need to be acknowledged, honoured, and validated. This begins by thinking things out on paper. Once your goal is written down, it allows you to step back and evaluate how important it actually is to you and how serious you are about it. Sometimes, this takes time. At first, every goal, dream, or desire is experienced a little bit like a passionate love affair. There is a little honeymoon phase, where the pursuit of the goal seems to be exciting, important, and glamourous. The beauty of having your goals written down is that you can return to this written record, over and over again. You will quickly filter through which goals are truly important to you and which goals are only whimsical.

6. The Power of Creating Achievement Frustration

Achievement frustration is a very powerful concept, and it is something that we can all relate to in everyday life. Have you ever identified something you wanted, and wanted it so badly, yet not had it? Were you frustrated? What you were experiencing was a type of achievement frustration, a psychological state of tension in which you are aware of the gap between your current reality and an expectation for something you'd like to achieve in the future.

Fortunately, this gap causes us a lot of psychological tension. For example, once you set a goal and you constantly remind yourself of your goal (which most people fail to do strategically), you begin to experience this frustration, or this gap in your reality of where you are now and where you want to be. Your brain will then do everything possible to close this gap and help create your desired reality. I believe this is what happened to me when I was writing daily about my aspirations to offer motivational speaking. It became so real in my mind that I had to make it happen. To not have made it happen would have been too discomforting and frustrating. Thus, it became necessary for me to close the gap between my current state and desire.

When you set a goal and review it frequently, you are motivated by the tension and frustration you experience as a result of not having achieved the goal yet. And you are also motivated by the future pleasure of actually achieving the goal.

The concept of writing goals down is not a new concept. In fact, we use this concept on a daily basis. For instance, we write to-do lists for our basic tasks and errands that we want to accomplish in a day. It's funny how basic the tasks are compared to our bigger, more complex dreams. However, many of us find making lists the best way to get organized and to ensure that all tasks are executed. If we need to write down our daily goals for such simple tasks, then you can bet that it would be an important idea to do the same for our bigger, more important dreams. Here's my favourite suggestion on how to organize this process.

START AN EVOLVING ACHIEVEMENTS BINDER

Organizing Your Brainstormed Ideas and Goals

All right, let's get you ready to start organizing all your ideas and potential goals for the future. You're going to want to keep a record of all your ideas for what you want to achieve. For years, I wasted so much time and money on buying pretty journals and notebooks for writing down my goals. I'd end up, not only writing down my goals, but I'd use these notebooks as a journal as well. So, my goals and other thoughts all became mixed up with no real functionality. Also, it became difficult to add in new goals, because I never knew where I left off previously. And there was no room to continue writing my goals, because I used that space to write about something completely unrelated. Likewise, if I wanted to take out or change my older goals, I'd have to rip pages out of my notebook, which of course had other unrelated, yet valuable information. In a nutshell, it was challenging to have all my various goals in different categories, because they were randomly scattered throughout too many notebooks. Of course, when these notebooks became full, I ended up throwing many of them out, because I had no need to keep all my journal entries, and I figured that I would just re-write all my goals in the next notebook that I would buy.

You can avoid all these problems by putting together an Evolving Achievements Binder. This is an easy-to-use, practical filing system that allows you to maintain, update, and delete pages as you see fit. You will devote this entire binder to your goals. Think of it as a landing place for your ideas, desires, and wants. The key is to capture your ideas, so that you can evaluate them at a later time. Here's what you'll need:

1) A nice three-ring binder
2) Lined paper to go inside your binder
3) Tabs or dividers

BENEFITS OF THE EVOLVING ACHIEVEMENTS BINDER

Because you are using a binder, whenever you want to add more information or goals to a category, all you need to do is open the rings and add more paper. It's so simple and easy to maintain, and since I've converted to using my Evolving Achievements Binder, I've never gone back to using journals for the purposes of organizing my goals. Also, having the dividers or tabs will allow you to organize your goals by various categories that make sense to you. Whenever you think of a new idea, you simply find the tab/divider that corresponds to that type of goal and add it.

From time to time, because we are busy woman, there will be phases in our life when we get sidetracked and abandon some of our goals. This is normal. When this happens, you can take comfort in knowing that at least all your goals are all organized in one spot, which will prevent you from misplacing and forgetting about your goals. It might sound a bit ludicrous to suggest that someone would forget about their goals, but it happens all the time. For instance, think of your to-do lists that you have. Imagine that you've written some of your errands on a few sheets of loose paper around the house. Some are in your journal, while others are on your calendar. When the list of errands is scattered all over the place, you are bound to misplace and thus forget about what you need to get done. You easily lose your focus. It's really no different with our goals. We need to keep them all organized in one place—a place where we can be sure to find them. This way, when a period of time goes by and you haven't attended to your goals, you'll be able to pick up right where you left off without any delays.

The Evolving Achievement Binder will also allow you to insert your plans for *how* you'll achieve your goals. Whenever you come across new resources, services, or other ideas about how you can achieve your goals, you'll insert them into the Planning Section of that category of goals. As we'll discuss later, once you have brainstormed and set your goals, you'll need to devise a general plan or at least outline some steps that will allow you to start taking action towards your goals. Just as people forget about their goals or get sidetracked, the same thing happens with their *plans* for achieving their goals, even though they are committed to their goals. They start taking action, and then they run into a few barriers. Once they get stuck, confused, or frustrated, they lose their focus and forget about their plan and abandon it. When your plan is written down, you'll never forget what your next steps are. If you have multiple plans written down, you will always have alternatives and something to return to, along with many other ideas of what you might try next to achieve your goals.

Every woman needs a serious organizational system that enables her to treasure her dreams and goals and to take them seriously.

Having a binder dedicated to achieving your goals will increase your confidence that you *can indeed* achieve those goals. The binder is like a concentrated source of energy that fuels your goals and propels you to take more and more action towards these goals. This happens because it provides you with a clarified focus. Everything you ever wanted to be, do, or achieve will be contained within this binder. The ideas have already been turned into something concrete and tangible. This helps you perceive and think about your goals more seriously just because you can see them. Then, the mere act of reading your goals over and over again imprints them deeper and deeper into your subconscious mind.

CHAPTER 3

The Dreamstorm

REFLECTING ON YOUR DREAMS AND GOALS

> Find out who you are and do it on purpose.
> -Dolly Parton

All right, the magical time has arrived. Grab your favourite java or tea and find a relaxing, peaceful, or inspiring environment—a place where you can spend a few uninterrupted hours with just you, a journal, and a pen. Your next step is to begin exploring your dreams and goals on paper. It is crucial that you complete these exercises before moving onto the next chapters of this book.

The initial process of setting goals includes an examination for what is possible in our life. Whom do we want to become? What do we want to do? What would we like to acquire? It is important for us to reflect upon all of the potential options that we might consider for what is possible in our life. When we are dreaming big, we are reflecting on our "possible self" (Markus & Nurius, 1986)—representations of our ideal future self, including our goals, hopes, and aspirations for our future. They are important because they provide us with motivation to become or do something different and make the necessary changes for our desired future. Our possible self acts as the bridge to link together our present and future selves. And when we take the time to explore our possible selves, we are in essence trying on different options for what we'd like to become (Dunkel, Kelts, & Coon, 2006). It sounds a bit like shopping for your ideal future self doesn't it? How much fun is that?

I have included five different categories to help you reflect upon your possible selves or potential goals. This is only one way to organize your potential goals. Don't worry if some of your goals overlap into different categories. This is normal and expected.

Do not allow yourself to get frustrated with organizing your goals into headings or categories. This type of perfectionism might keep you paralyzed from ever progressing. What is more important is to simply get started and to write your ideas down on paper. Here are the five general categories to get you started:

1. **Health / Wellness**
2. **Career / Lifestyle**
3. **Money**
4. **Personal Development / Leisure**
5. **Relationships / Spirituality**

Health includes your overall well-being, along with your fitness and nutrition. Career and Lifestyle includes goals related to working, running a business, and finding work-life balance. Money refers to your investments, budgets, and anything materialistic that you are looking to purchase. The fourth category includes goals for intellectual and personal development, continuing education, as well as any recreation and leisure preferences. Finally, relationships refer to your relationship with yourself, including your emotional, mental, and spiritual health. It also includes relationships with other people.

Turn ahead to the following pages and get started with your "dreamstorm" now. Within each section, I've included a list of questions to help you reflect on what types of goals might be important to you.

HEALTH GOALS

> *Fitness—if it came in a bottle, everybody would have a great body.*
> *-Cher*

I believe that our health is one of the most important areas of our life, because without our health, it is difficult to enjoy our own life and the company of others. Also, our energy and health have a direct impact on our levels of success. If there is any inspiring story to motivate you to set goals with respect to your health, it's the story of Taisha Hayes.

Taisha grew up with a love of food and an aversion to exercise, so much so that by the time she was twenty-three years old, she weighed nearly three hundred pounds. While she never really envisioned herself as obese, she told herself that "someday" she would lose weight. At age twenty-three, she hit rock bottom and was determined to lose the weight.

When Taisha set her weight loss goals, she focused on making progress in increments, taking small steps, one at a time. She knew that in order to lose one hundred and thirty pounds, she was going to need to be consistent and focus on taking small steps over time. Her philosophy was to focus on her actions and habits as opposed to an end weight, which was far into the future. In the short term, Taisha stayed motivated and focused by setting a simple goal of dropping one dress size at a time.

Before Taisha started exercising, she was a complete couch potato, so she began exercising to videos for thirty minutes per day in the comfort of her home. As a result, she began to burn more calories. She focused on cutting out liquid calories and gradually eating fewer and fewer calories per day. She found new and healthy recipes that she could integrate into her diet, one at a time, and she found a way to eat healthy recipes that she actually enjoyed. It was an exhilarating feeling to accomplish finding a meal plan she loved and one that helped her shed weight.

Perhaps the most important step for Taisha was creating the right mindset for success. She constantly reminded herself that she could achieve her goals, and that she was no different than any other person who had lost weight. She also reminded herself that she deserved to be happy and healthy. Whenever Taisha had a setback with her diet or exercise program, she accepted it immediately and focused on making a positive choice at her next meal, or she made sure that she started working out the next day. She never interpreted her mistakes or setbacks as permanent, but as a normal part of the process. Her mistakes were simply a cue to pick herself up and keep going. Over the course of a year, Taisha lost one hundred pounds, losing an additional thirty pounds gradually, as her fitness improved. Taisha has successfully kept the weight off for over seven years!

Taisha shares her motivational weight loss solutions on her website, www.THayesFitness.com, and runs a successful business as a personal trainer. After being featured as a guest on the *Dr. Oz Show*, Taisha was invited to join his team of Wellness Warriors and now writes a blog, sharing her health and fitness tips on the *Dr. Oz Show* website. Most recently, Taisha has created her own DVD workout series.

Movement is a medicine for creating change
in a person's physical, emotional, and mental states.
—Carol Welch

Wow! Talk about motivation! If Taisha Hayes can do this, so can you! Regardless of what your health goals are, I'm sure this story can inspire you to put your health first. Here are some questions below to get you thinking about what types of goals you might want to set.

POWER QUESTIONS

General Health

1. What does having excellent health mean to you? Your definition of health will be different than anyone else's. Define it now.
2. When it comes to your health, what do you value the most? What are your health values, and how will you satisfy them?
3. What does having excellent hygiene mean to you? How is your overall hygiene? Do you put off visiting the dentist? Are you in the habit of taking good care of your teeth and flossing daily?
4. Do you have any health concerns that you've delayed visiting a doctor for? What other checkups might you need? Do you need to have any particular concerns addressed by any type of specialized doctor?
5. Do you need to supplement your diet with a multivitamin or mineral complex? I can remember that for years, I never believed that supplements did anything for me. I had tried many different ones and never felt a difference in my symptoms. Then, one year, several months went by and I felt completely fatigued. I would come home from work and need to go almost directly to bed to rest. I was exhausted and constantly had dizzy spells. Recalling that my previous blood tests indicated I was low in vitamin B12 and iron, I decided to give these supplements a fair shot. Literally, within forty-eight hours, it felt as though a switch was turned on in my body. My energy came back full force. Even though I was already consuming plenty of vitamin B12 in my diet, I wasn't absorbing it. So, don't be afraid to be open to trying a professional's suggestion about which supplements you need to take. It can make a world of difference in your well-being and energy.
6. How are your sleeping routines? Do you need to commit to getting more sleep (or less)?
7. Are you in need of any services from health or alternative health care practitioners? For example, maybe you've been

struggling with knee or back pain and you assume that nothing will help. Have you really tried everything? Perhaps you'll consult with an athletic therapist who can analyze the exact problem that your body is experiencing while jogging or walking, for example. Or maybe you need to visit a podiatrist to get fitted for a pair of orthotics that fit your shoes nicely. This, too, can eliminate back-, hip-, knee-, and foot-related pain. Maybe you need to find a new physiotherapist who can help you recover. The longer you leave an injury, the more you risk making it worse. Address your injuries or discomforts today and tap into a professional's expertise, one who deals with these types of problems every day. Many of us don't achieve our goals, because we give up when we don't have a solution within us. You don't need to have all the answers yourself. It's not possible.

The point is don't give up and don't assume that nothing can help. Keep looking. Make a commitment today to not give up on staying active. Facing physical barriers and handling injuries is an expected experience in one's healthy lifestyle that many women will experience. Most people use their injuries as an excuse. Don't do that. Think of the cost of these services as a good insurance policy against ill health, weight gain, and irritability. You are worth it.

Fitness

1. How many times a week do you expect yourself to exercise? For how long each time will you exercise in total?
2. Do you want to increase the strength of your muscles or become more toned? How many sets and repetitions within each set do you need to do?
3. Do you want to increase your cardiovascular fitness? How long will your aerobic sessions last?
4. Have you considered building a home gym? What exercise equipment or exercise DVDs would you buy?

5. Do you need an iPod or Mp3 player to listen to music as you exercise? What new music do you want?
6. Would you like to hire a personal trainer who can customize a fitness routine for you?
7. What new items do you need to purchase to motivate yourself more or to make your exercise more convenient? For example, consider the following:

- iPod or Mp3 player to listen to music
- Up-to-date music from iTunes to download onto your music player
- Workout clothes
- Pair of shoes for jogging and walking
- Gym bag
- Portable notebook to track your workout details
- Pedometer to measure the distance or steps taken
- Water bottle for the gym
- Waist pouch to carry your keys, notebook, or other items

8. How can you expand your current exercise routines to include more variety? Do you want to try something different such as yoga, tai chi, or kickboxing? Do you want to go hiking or try power walking? Do you want to join a recreational sports team or try a different type of athletic activity? Here are some common physical activities that you might consider:

- Bicycling or mountain biking
- Train for a triathlon: running, biking, and swimming
- Brisk walking
- Jogging
- Train to run a marathon
- Swimming
- Aqua-aerobics at your local aquatic centre
- Jumping on a mini-trampoline
- Yoga or pilates
- Aerobics classes at your local gym

- Workout videos in the privacy of your own home
- Golf
- Rollerblading
- Skating
- Tennis
- Squash
- Soccer
- Volleyball
- Basketball
- Rowing
- Hiking along a river or mountain
- Martial arts
    - Kempo
    - Karate
    - Tai kwon doe
    - Kung-fu
    - Kick-boxing

Nutrition and Eating

1. What types of habits do you need to quit?

- Snacking
- Eating junk food
- Smoking
- Drinking alcohol
- Caffeine intake
- Eating fast food
- Eating meat
- Mindless social eating

2. What types of healthy habits do you want to adopt?

- Eat more living, raw foods
- Become a vegetarian or a vegan
- Drink more water

- Plan and pack a healthy lunch for work each day
- Eat a salad each day
- Eat a large serving of vegetables with dinner
- Take multivitamins each day
- Eat smaller portions
- Increase protein in your diet
- Decrease refined carbohydrates
- Engage in meal planning
- Plan ahead of time meals that you'll eat at restaurants
- Buy groceries at a pre-determined time each week
- Keep a food journal to record what you eat

3. What type of professional assistance will you need to help you achieve your eating and nutrition goals? For example, do you prefer to join a weight loss clinic for social support or meal planning assistance? What about hiring a personal nutritionist?
4. What types of books or courses would you seek out to help you achieve your eating goals? Would you buy some new healthy recipe books? Would you take a healthy cooking class?
5. Do you need to purchase any plastic containers or other items to pack and transport all of your healthy home-cooked meals? Consider any of the following:

- A 2L water bottle
- Ice packs
- Large lunch bag
- Oversized container for a salad
- Mini container to put salad dressing in
- A mini padded bag for utensils

6. What fitness model or sports celebrity would you like to emulate? For what reasons?
7. What measurements do you want your body to have? For example, what size of pants do you want to be able to fit into? How much do you want to weigh? What do you

want your body measurements and your body fat levels to reside at?

Stress Management and Self-care Goals

How can you achieve peace of mind and reduce the stress in your life? What do you need for self-care? For example, what sorts of activities do you need to incorporate into your life? Consider the following for ideas:

- Journalling
- Reading a book or magazine for pure leisure
- Soaking in a hot tub with candles
- Taking a nap
- Meditation
- Prayer
- Deep breathing
- Spending time with friends
- Listening to relaxing music
- Going for a nice walk
- Massage
- Seeking out a counsellor
- Reiki
- Energy therapy
- Aromatherapy / burning of incense
- Chiropractor
- Going to a drum circle
- Reflexology
- Acupuncture
- Hypnotherapy
- Visualization
- Visiting a naturopathic doctor

What routines or habits in the past have helped you to relax and simply feel good about yourself and your life? What types of goals will you set to integrate these routines into your life? What new health and wellness approaches could change your life in a positive way? Which habits would make you feel like a million bucks? Write down your health goals in your journal now.

CAREER GOALS

Careers come in all sizes, shapes, and forms for women these days. There truly is no limit! Also, more and more women are becoming entrepreneurial with respect to their careers. After reading the follow story of an amazing woman I interviewed, I'm sure you'll have your own entrepreneurial ideas that might inspire your career path.

Never work just for money or for power.
They won't save your soul or help you sleep at night.
-Marian Wright Edelman

As an entrepreneurial spirit her entire life, Rachael Smith, started off her career as a first grade teacher, creating new and creative curricula for her students. While she enjoyed this career, things took a surprising turn shortly after the birth of her second child. With two active toddlers, Rachael found herself a busy mom, travelling around the city, trying to complete her many errands and care for the needs of her children.

One day, Rachael was flying with her two children to Tucson. As they made their way onto the plane, Rachael's daughter cried for her bottle, while her son demanded his toy train. She shuffled through a large, dishevelled bag full of many supplies and toys and became frustrated when she pulled out a bottle that was dripping everywhere. She had to dump out her entire bag just to find her son's toy train. Being a teacher, who prefers being super organized, Rachael was dissatisfied and frustrated. In this moment, she began her journey as an "accidental entrepreneur." As a mom, she had a burning desire to solve her problem of being disorganized.

Over the course of the next six months, Rachael tossed around ideas about how she could design her own organized bag for mothers. She began from scratch by grabbing a few boxes and some duct tape and worked outside in her backyard where she created her own practical model. Rachael even made sure that her model bag had drawers. Slowly, but surely, she designed a model of an innovative bag from a cardboard box.

After much experimenting, she went to the library and signed out a book that taught her how to find a manufacturer who could build a prototype of her bag. After a year of working closely with a manufacturer, Rachael's first bag prototype was finished, but it wasn't what she expected—the size was too big. As she tweaked her design further, she found it important to talk to other women to learn about their preferences. After all, if she was going to invest more time and money into her product line, she had to go right to the source—her future customers. So, Rachael roamed around the parks where mothers gathered and carried with her different types of material to get their feedback. She also held parties in her home to gather ideas and to ensure that her product line would be in demand. Rachael was concerned about long-standing quality and creating a product line of bags that she would be proud of, as opposed to prematurely rushing an order of bags to production.

In the meantime, Rachael took another brave step forward. Despite her bags not being quite finished the way she wanted, she signed up for the ABC Kids Show in Las Vegas to display her bags. It was there that she met a man who was so intrigued with her product that he demanded she send him her bag prototype, so that he could put the finishing touches on her bag line. So, it was a done deal! After almost three years of persistently pursuing this endeavour and taking small steps forward, Rachael's product line of bags went public and her sales began to take off. Rachael was so successful that she had the chance to display her bags at the Emmy's, where she sparked great interest with various celebrities. Rachael now has over five different bag designs with many different types of colourful vibrant fabrics. She is constantly taking small steps to improve her product line, always trying to stay on the cutting edge. Best of all, Rachael enjoys being able to pursue such meaningful work.

Even though it was a long journey and there were times when Rachael put it all aside, she picked herself back up and told herself that she would never quit. She always exercised her faith and took time to reflect on the reason she was doing it all—to give back to other moms and simplify their lives in a fashionable, fun, and convenient way. You can view Rachael Smith's product line of bags by visiting her website at www.mrssmithbags.com

Feeling inspired yet to start thinking about your own career goals? Read through the following questions to give you more ideas, just in case.

POWER QUESTIONS

You have to do what you love to do, not get stuck in that comfort zone of a regular job. Life is not a dress rehearsal. This is it.
-Lucinda Basset

General Lifestyle

1. What do you want to become and create in your lifetime?
2. What do you want to experience?
3. How do you want to focus your time and energy?
4. What is your life purpose, mission, or vision?
5. What does your ideal lifestyle look like? How can you stimulate your mind to think of creative, new ways for how to improve your lifestyle?
6. When you think of your past, what have you been doing and what was happening around you during the times when you became more creative, gathered new insights or ideas about living your life, or embarked upon new and exciting goals? Which of these circumstances do you want to re-create?

7. What do you find yourself daydreaming and fantasizing about with respect to your career?
8. How can you raise your standards for how you want to live your life?
9. What expectations have you always held for your life, but haven't yet attended to?
10. What are your favourite hobbies? Is there a way to integrate any of them into your career?
11. Which environments are most stimulating and refreshing to your mind?
12. What lifestyle rituals, activities, or habits make you feel good about yourself?

Vocational Goals

> *The woman who can create her own job*
> *is the woman who will win fame and fortune.*
> *-Amelia Earhart*

1. What sorts of activities are you so passionate about that you would gladly get up at 5:30 a.m. to start them? In other words, what gets you most excited in life? What have you always been extremely passionate about?
2. What would you do with yourself if you knew that you couldn't fail?
3. Where do you want to be five years down the road with respect to your career? Ten years? Twenty years?
4. If you had all the knowledge needed, what projects, activities, or businesses would you start?
5. What are you most talented at? What sorts of skills seem to come naturally to you?
6. What do you believe is really unique about you that makes you stand out from others?
7. What have other people told you is unique about you? What hints do your friends, colleagues, and family give you regarding

what they believe you are good at, or what direction you should head in?

8. What other skills would you like to develop in your career?
9. What courses, certificates, diplomas, or degrees might you pursue that would make you more marketable?
10. What type of business do you see yourself owning?
11. If you had to work in a society where 1) there was no pay, and 2) you had to create your own work and/or services for the community, what would you do? The purpose of this question is to help you think about what you are naturally interested in when the influence of monetary rewards is taken away.
12. If you have a business, are you looking to expand or improve some aspect of it? What sorts of activities will you do yourself, and which tasks could be outsourced to someone else?
13. How can you increase your personal business revenue?
14. How can you create a better work-life balance?
15. What kind of personal brand and reputation could you work on building for your own career?
16. What personal achievements do you want to see happen over the course of your lifelong career? Imagine that you are one hundred years old, sitting in your "rocking-chair," looking back on your career. What is important and satisfying to know that you've achieved?
17. Find someone in the community who evidences what you want to become. Ask if he or she is willing to be your professional mentor.
18. What organizations or associations could you join for the purposes of fulfilling your career goals?
19. Is it time for a change in your career?
20. How could you keep yourself better organized at work? Do you need to clean out your office or re-arrange it? Do you need to create better filing systems either electronically or paper-based? Do you need to delete your old emails? Do you need shelves or bulletin boards?
21. How might you create a more aesthetically pleasing environment at work? Would you like new artwork, plants,

air fresheners, or new desk accessories? Do you need better lighting? Does your office need to be de-cluttered?

MONEY GOALS

> There is nothing wrong with saying,
> "I want to have more,"
> "I want to be more,"
> "I did this for money."
> -Suze Orman

For most of us women, I'm sure we could all use more money. After all, it makes our life easier and can provide convenient solutions to some of the typical problems we might encounter, e.g., putting our children through school. Also, let's face it—with money, we can afford many luxuries that we might not otherwise be able to experience. Finally, it's possible that your goals with respect to money are to simply pay down your debt. Read Jaime Tardy's story on how something as simple as this changed her life.

Jaime Tardy worked at a corporate job as a project manager earning six figures, travelling around the country, and more often than not, working long hours. While she was "getting by," she knew in the back of her mind that there was more to life than her job. She couldn't imagine herself staying at her job long term, because she wanted to start a family, and this type of lifestyle wouldn't be sustainable for her and her family.

After a lot of soul searching and journalling, she began to set a few important life goals. Her aim was to pay off her debt of 70k before the birth of her first child. A second goal was to find a job that would provide her with work-life balance, and a job that she'd be so passionate about that she would wake up Monday mornings excited to start her day. A third goal was to start the journey towards becoming a millionaire.

Jaime broke down her goals into concrete action steps. First, she had to calculate how much debt she had. In addition, she wanted to get her husband's buy-in and make sure that he, too, would be as committed as she was to paying down the debt. Rather than just taking very small steps in paying down the debt, Jaime and her husband decided to sell their older jeep, a brand new car, and several of their other belongings to make some immediate payments on their debt.

Her husband took on a second job, and Jaime took on extra hours in her job to speed up the process. In fact, when Jaime was seven months pregnant, there were times when she was working twenty-four hours consecutively. One of Jaime's biggest challenges was that she was so frugal and budget-oriented that she constantly had to set limits and say "no" to some of the activities her friends invited her to. Friends and family asked her why she couldn't afford certain activities, and she had to explain that her goal was to pay off all of her debt before the birth of her first child. At times, she felt isolated and frustrated by her self-imposed limits, but she knew it would be worth it once she achieved her goal. Talk about determination!

Jaime kept herself focused on finding a job that she would be passionate about. She set a goal to open up her own business. She also motivated herself by joining a mastermind group, which constantly reminded her of how much she wanted to work for herself. In addition, having a mentor was very important and the support she received helped her understand that she wasn't the only one experiencing a tough journey on the way towards her goals. According to Jaime, it is completely normal and expected to experience a tough journey—otherwise, if it were that easy, everyone would achieve their life goals.

As a result of Jaime's major efforts and getting her husband on board, they were able to pay down 5k on their debt each month, and within one and a half years, they paid off the entire 70k. She wasn't far from her original goal of having the debt paid off by the time her son was born. At the time their 70k was paid off, her son was only four months old. Shortly after, Jaime was able to quit her full-time job as a project manager. By that time, she and her husband had already accumulated 20k in savings.

Jaime eventually opened a successful personal and business coaching practice that allows her to work part-time. She's in love with her current job and enjoys having time with her family. Last but not least, Jaime is on the road to achieving her goal of becoming a millionaire. You, too, can be inspired from her journey by visiting http://eventualmillionaire.com. Be sure to listen to her free podcasts where she interviews people who have reached millionaire status.

POWER QUESTIONS

Do what you love and the money will follow.
-Marsha Sinetar

Savings and Investments

1. How much money do you want to save on a weekly, biweekly, or monthly basis?
2. What do you plan to invest your money in? A savings account? Your retirement 401k or RRSP plan? Are you considering investing in penny stocks, starting your own brokerage account, or buying or trading options?
3. What professionals do you need to consult with, if any, to get your finances in order?
4. Which books and subject areas on finance/money would you like to learn more about? Are there any magazines that you'd like to subscribe to?
5. What debt would you like to pay off, and how much will you pay off each week or month?
6. What sorts of purchases would you like to cut back on? What is unnecessary? Out of all the things you buy, which items give you the greatest return on your investment?
7. How might a budgeting chart or spreadsheet help you to keep track of your finances?
8. Do you want to create a passive income? What goals would you set around that?

Spending and Materialistic Goals

1. What purchases would you like to make?

2. Are you thinking of purchasing a new home, pool, or car?
3. Are you hoping to buy yourself a new wardrobe?
4. Are you interested in hiring an interior decorator to enhance your environment at home?
5. What would you buy if money wasn't an issue for you? Write it down!

PERSONAL DEVELOPMENT GOALS

> It's not enough to be good if you have the ability to be better. It is not enough to be very good if you have the ability to be great.
> -Alberta Lee Cox

I don't know about you, but without personal development in my own life, I'd feel so stagnant and dry. Developing my intellectual pursuits and stimulating my mind is one of my greatest pleasures in life. Also, our personal development pursuits often affect our career paths. Consider the story of this brilliant woman I interviewed, Laurel Clark.

Dr. Laurel Clark is the President of the School of Metaphysics, an ordained minister in the Interfaith Church of Metaphysics, an intuitive counsellor, and a teacher of metaphysics since 1979. Laurel didn't start off with grand, lofty goals. She always wanted to be a writer, but she wasn't attached to particular outcomes, such as fame or becoming a published author and international speaker. Instead, she related more to having an overarching vision of helping others. It was this ideal that guided her efforts in achieving success with her writing and personal development.

Since the age of five, Laurel had the idea to write a book. As a child, she created small handmade books and started her own newspaper. For years, she journalled, kept a diary, and wrote reflective pieces related to personal growth. Writing a book seemed like a much bigger project, one too big to tackle. Instead, she developed a collection of articles, essays, and short pieces of writing that centered on the methods she had learned for self-improvement: meditation, dream interpretation, concentration, and visualization. Writing short articles was infinitely more manageable than writing a full-length book, which seemed so daunting!

Laurel's articles and essays grew from her experience as a student of metaphysics. She had been developing concentration, practicing meditation, and other mental exercises, and this was causing her to become much calmer, more clear, and relaxed with herself. She wanted to help others learn such skills and to be inspired to change themselves. In fact, Laurel had grown to understand that being an example was the best way to influence others. People who knew her well remarked that she seemed more decisive and self-assured, as she developed these mental skills. Laurel wanted to share this knowledge with other people, so that they could make similar changes.

Laurel discovered that writing brought her fulfillment, because she learned more about her studies during the process. At the same time, her confidence began to increase.

One day, Laurel asked herself, *How can I reach a larger audience with my writing?* She was fortunate to have excellent teachers and mentors who encouraged her. So, she began to research to find various publications, such as magazines, newspapers, and journals that would publish her work. Through trial and error, Laurel persisted and found a number of magazines that published her articles.

After her first piece of writing was published, she experienced a snowball effect and gained momentum with her writing. Her confidence increased further, and eventually, she decided it was time to write that book she'd dreamed about since childhood. At first, her inner voice chided, *Who am I to publish a book?* A book was a much bigger project than writing short articles. Laurel realized that the key to her success would be to chunk her goal down into small steps. Doing so made the process similar to writing a collection of small pieces with a related theme.

Alongside Laurel's writing were her speaking engagements, another way she carried out her vision to help others improve their life through developing practical skills in visualization, concentration, dream interpretation, and meditation. She started off small, developing her speaking skills in university and college classrooms and smaller lecture venues, including the Rotary and Optimist clubs and various networking groups.

Laurel's progression led her from teacher to director to area director to regional director at the School of Metaphysics. Now, she's the national president! She also teaches and speaks to international corporations like IBM, Eli Lilly, and Hilton Hotels. She has published several books, including *The Law of Attraction and Other Secrets of Visualization*. Laurel understands her journey as an ongoing process in which she needs to keep learning, growing, and making a difference in people's lives. You can learn more about Dr. Laurel Clark by visiting http://www.som.org/NewPages/Newsite07/SOMNavigation/BoardMembers/ClarkLaurel.html

Obviously, whatever you choose for your personal development pursuits will shape who you become as a person, and, possibly even your career! The possibilities are endless, really. Consider the following questions to inspire some further ideas on how you'd like to expand your context.

POWER QUESTIONS

Personal Development

1. What are your favourite topics of conversation? How can you further engage yourself in these topic areas? Are there particular books to read, or certain like-minded people you want to meet?
2. Would you like to learn more words and increase your vocabulary?
3. Are there new languages you are hoping to learn?
4. Would you like to subscribe to any particular newspapers or magazines that really interest you? And would you like to schedule time in your calendar to ensure that you have time to read these publications?

5. Do you want to write articles, poems, short stories, fiction, or non-fiction novels? Do you want to write scripts for music, plays, or movies? How will you get this process started? Will you read a how-to book, attend a seminar, or hire a consultant to help you?
6. What other learning and/or intellectual pursuits do you want to embrace to keep your mind fresh?

Leisure / Recreation

1. What little pleasures or "extras" in life do you crave, but never seem to make the time for? What are they?
2. What creative pursuits interest you? Do you want to learn to paint or create sculptures? Do you want to journal on a regular basis? Do you want to begin scrapbooking? Do you have a desire to decorate your house or paint a room?
3. Would you like to volunteer within your community? What types of volunteer work would create the best "win-win" situations?
4. What things would you like to do in your life to have more fun? How might you create more adventure in your life?
5. What types of vacations would you like to go on? Where would you like to travel to?
6. What are your favourite hobbies that you would like to make more time for?
7. Do you have a desire to write a personal biography or life story?
8. Have you thought about researching your genealogy?
9. Do you want to create photo albums or scrapbooks to pass onto anyone in your family?

RELATIONSHIPS AND SPIRITUALITY

> It is easier to live through someone else than to become complete yourself.
> -Betty Friedan

Last, but not least, I believe it is wise to set goals with respect to our relationships with others and to ourself. The latter is what I refer to as our spirituality—our relationship to ourself. We are all on a journey getting to know ourself better, exploring meaning and finding our purpose. I was particularly inspired when Leta Hamilton shared her story with me, and I'm sure you'll feel inspired also. It's another great example of how nurturing one area of our life can positively impact another area of our life.

Leta Hamilton's goal was to find a sense of spirituality and inner peace during motherhood. Early on in Leta's life, she held the image of herself as a woman in a high-powered career earning lots of money. Once she had children, however, that image changed. She was forced to redefine how she measured her self-worth and how she defined personal success. Up until the birth of her first infant, she had been working as a highly paid executive assistant to a CEO in the private equity industry. She had expected that she would find a sense of inner peace and fulfillment by having a prestigious high paying job, but it failed to meet her needs.

With the birth of her second child, the opportunity to become a full-time, stay-at-home mom arose. Initially, Leta was relieved not to have to go to an office everyday, as she thought that spending her days in the company of her children would fulfill her in ways that her office jobs never did. Along with full-time motherhood came a set of experiences she wasn't prepared for. What a surprise when full-time motherhood didn't grant her a sense of inner peace. Leta was slowly learning that she couldn't develop her spiritual self and find fulfillment through any of her external circumstances.

Something deep inside told her that motherhood could be an honourable, incredibly spiritual path and that it was possible to be a mother and still have an inner core of peace, which no amount of ninja fighting, tantrums, dirty diapers, peas all over the floor, or interrupted nights of sleep could ever tear apart. In search of this, she began taking steps to read every self-help and spiritual growth book she could get her hands on. All of them were wonderful, but none of them seemed relevant to her as a mom of active and boisterous one—and three-year-old boys. In total frustration, she decided to stop looking externally in books for answers. Instead, she began reflecting and writing about the spiritual lessons and insights she was learning from her experiences with her children—ones that would eventually lead her to inner peace and fulfillment.

By observing her children's actions, they taught her what it is like to be completely present, live in the moment, and experience authentic joy and disappointment. Watching them play, she learned about the magic of creativity and the power of the imagination. They also taught her how to develop and practice patience, forbearance, perseverance, and resilience to withstand the storms of life. Most of all, they taught her what unconditional love is.

Through these observations and writing about her personal insights, Leta learned that motherhood was a test to maintain an inner sense of peace no matter what her external circumstances were. As she began to feel more in touch with her own spirituality and sense of purpose, interesting things began to happen. Though Leta had developed a manuscript on her learning lessons, a third pregnancy and a home move kept her manuscript on hold for two years. Eventually, with the prodding of a friend, she dusted off the manuscript and set a goal to become a published author.

She now has a radio show, "The Way of the Toddler Hour," that is broadcast to listeners from London to Seattle. She also speaks in front of business, parenting, and moms' groups about what our children can teach us about finding peace even in the midst of dirty diapers and piles of laundry. While it is still an ongoing journey, Leta's deep and abiding faith that motherhood is a spiritual path in and of itself keeps her moving forward to greater unknown ventures. You can learn more about Leta Hamilton by visiting www.letahamilton.com

This story was truly touching—an amazing example of how when we nurture the deep parts of our soul that are yearning for purpose and meaning, we can often end up finding clarity and even success in other parts of our life.

So, what would you like to focus on with respect to your spirituality? Also, what about your relationships to others?

POWER QUESTIONS

Relationship to Self

Be a first rate version of yourself,
not a second rate version of someone else.
-Judy Garland

1. What have you always wanted to give or do for yourself, but never had the courage for?
2. How are you nurturing your own spirituality? What, if any, are your religious pursuits? How are you nurturing your faith? What could be improved upon?
3. In what situations, and with which people do you need to set firmer boundaries?
4. What type of relationships do you want in your life that will directly or indirectly inspire and encourage you to achieve your dreams?
5. What needs healing within you? Does your mental, emotional, or psychological health need attention? For what? What negative patterns need the attention of a professional counsellor or coach?

Family

1. What kind of family do you want to create? Do you want children? What type of parent do you want to be? What kind of partner do you want to be? What kind of brother,

sister, grandmother, grandfather do you want to be known as?
2. Do you want to spend more time with your family? What sorts of activities would you do with your family?
3. How could you be more generous or giving towards your family? What acts of kindness could you embrace?
4. What gifts would you like to be able to give, and what deeds would you like to offer, and to whom?
5. Do you need to connect with others more often? What types of social functions, family reunions, or other celebrations could you host in your own home or organize elsewhere? How could you make the get-together really special or fun for everyone? How could you surprise your guests?

Spousal and Partner Goals

1. What thoughtful things could you do that would make your significant other or partner feel really loved? Are there certain household chores that you could easily do for your partner? What would your partner appreciate most? Could you surprise your partner by making his or her favourite dinner? Could you pack his or her lunch for work? Could you take your partner out on a surprise date? Would you consider writing your partner nice, thoughtful, or romantic emails or letters on a regular basis? Would you want to stop by your partner's workplace and surprise him or her with a nice snack, meal, or coffee?
2. What could you do for your partner or family member that he or she would never expect you to do, or didn't think you would do?
3. How might you make a better point of asking about your partner's day, and his or her thoughts and feelings?
4. Do you need to make more time for your partner in general, e.g., by creating a "date night"?

Friendship Goals

1. What types of social gatherings could you plan with one or several of your friends? What is something special that you could do for your friend?
2. Do you need to become better at staying in touch with any of your friends?
3. Do you want to make more time for your friends, and make sure that you see or talk to them more often?
4. Are you looking to expand your social circle and meet new people? How are you going to do that? Could you join a club, association, or go to conferences based on some of your key interests?
5. Do you need to take acquaintances' invites up more on social functions? Are you making yourself approachable enough?

CHAPTER 4

Prioritize Your Passions

PRIORITIZE YOUR PASSIONS AND GET FOCUSED

> It's how we spend our time here and now that really matters. If you are fed up with the way you have come to interact with time, change it.
> -Marcia Weider

So, are you completely jazzed and excited after your dreamstorm session? Wait a minute. Now that you're full of ideas for what's possible, how will you decide what to focus on? Perhaps you have so many big dreams, goals, and ideas that you feel scattered, or you can't decide which goals deserve your focus immediately. Many people get very excited about their dreams, and then after they write them down, they lose focus. Your task is to decide which of your many dreams you should focus on now.

CAN I FOCUS ON MANY GOALS ALL AT ONCE?

The truth is, yes you can. Research has indicated that as long as your goals do not conflict, you can pursue multiple goals at the same time (Locke & Latham, 1990). You might be wondering how effective you can really be at pursuing all of your goals.

In order for you to achieve all of your goals, a certain degree of self-regulation is necessary. This refers to your ability to monitor your behaviours and actions towards your goal, and adjust them as necessary. It has been noted that one's self-regulation ability is limited, as it requires a great deal of energy to constantly monitor, track, and adjust one's behaviours (Muraven & Baumeister, 2000). Obviously, the more time you invest in one goal, the less time you have to invest in your other goals.

Lack of self-regulation and available attention or focus are major contributing factors to people giving up on their goals. According to goal-setting research, you can overcome this dilemma if you can learn to automate the action steps or habits involved in pursuing your goals, so that they don't require a lot of conscious effort (Koestner, 2008). There is a big difference between taking big leaps towards your goals versus baby steps. It's always easier to create and automate smaller, easy action steps and habits, than it is to suddenly get in the habit of making major changes and being able to stick to them. We'll discuss this further when we talk about changing behaviours. The question is, how quickly do you want to see results and success with your goals? The more you're in a hurry, the more you should focus and invest more time into that one important goal. Over time, as your habits become effortless, you might then decide to introduce other goals when you have the time and energy needed.

WHAT SHOULD I FOCUS ON FIRST?

Now that you have actually identified and written down many of your lifelong dreams and goals, you can evaluate how important each of them is to you. Obviously, *all* of these ideas are important to you in *some way*. They are practical, will increase your self-esteem, and satisfy lifelong dreams, or they might increase your prestige. However, not all of these intentions are going to be of equal importance to you *in this exact moment or time of your life.*

Your job is to figure out where to begin now. Which goals are a priority to you *right now*? Which goals would *excite* or energize you if you started them right now? Which goals are most important to achieve in the short-term versus the long-term? Below, I've suggested a few ways to help you identify your most important goals that you should get started with now.

STRATEGIES FOR FOCUSING ON YOUR MOST IMPORTANT GOAL

> *You CAN have it all. You just can't have it all at once.*
> *-Oprah Winfrey*

There are many different ways to prioritize which goals you should start focusing on now. Consider the following techniques.

Your objective is to identify the most important goals (one or two) in each category to get started with. Once you've done this, you will be more motivated to achieve those goals.

1. Rate each goal on a scale of 1 to 10, with 1 meaning that the goal is extremely important to you *right now at this exact moment in your life*, and 10 meaning that it is not a priority right now. Another way to think about this is that 1 means the goal is very important in the short-term, while 10 means it is *not* important in the short-term. After you have completed this step with your goals in each category, review the goals that you marked with a 1 or 2. Next, rank these goals in order of importance to give you a clear idea of which goal you should get started with now.
2. Another way to evaluate the importance of your goals is to write down the time by which you seriously would like to have accomplished the goal. This might give you an idea of what needs to be started *right now*. You might think in the following increments:

- One Week
- One Month
- Six Months
- One Year
- Five Years
- Ten Years
- Twenty Years

Obviously, the shorter the timeline, the more important the goal is to you at this time.

REFLECTIVE QUESTIONS TO HELP YOU PRIORITIZE

If you're still lacking clarity on which goals are most important to pursue, I've created a separate list of questions that will encourage you to reflect and to get in tune with what is important to you right now. Try asking yourself the following questions:

1. Which goals interest you the most? In other words, which goals do you think about the most?
2. What do you want to be known for professionally? This question came to me as an epiphany when I was trying to prioritize some of my own goals. I remember wanting to accomplish so many goals all at once. I was considering a counselling practice, real estate and stock market investments, ecommerce opportunities, publishing personal development books, and the list went on.

   Suddenly, it occurred to me—*What do I want to be known for? What do I want people to see me as an expert in? What am I most comfortable being an expert in? Real estate and finance? Or my expertise as it relates to helping people make changes and achieve goals?* My realization and decision at the time was to combine my passion for psychology, counselling, and goal setting to create a website. This became the goal that I focused on in my spare time, as opposed to the other financial pursuits. Now, don't get me wrong. This is not to say that I've neglected my financial goals. Rather, they are not a pursuit that I work at every single day.

3. If a genie could grant you three wishes in life, what would you wish for? The answer to this question can give you a good idea of what your top priorities are.
4. Which goals give you a heavy or lethargic sensation when you think about them, and which goals give you a "rush" when you think about them? Which goal(s) would give you the most energy if you could commit to it now?

   You'll find that as you review your list of brainstormed goals, there will be some goals that make you feel a bit apprehensive, lethargic, or will give you a heavy sensation in your body. This might be a clue that it's not the right goal or that it's a complex goal requiring many other barriers to be dealt with. For instance, many times when I would try to buckle down and get serious about some of my financial investment goals, I would feel a bit lost, confused, and anxious about my potential decision to move forward. It felt a bit "scary" in a way. I felt as though I needed to really push myself down a road that I wasn't totally comfortable with.

A lot of this had to do with the fact that I lacked information to give me the reassurance I needed. I've recognized that while some of these goals are important, they will take more time and effort, and will be pursued when the timing is more convenient. In addition, they will be goals that will require me to draw on the outside knowledge of an expert in that field. Otherwise, I have many more exciting possibilities to focus on that offer me a lot of energy, passion, and far greater rewards in my life.

5. If someone close to you read your list of goals, which goals would they choose as being most typical of who you are? Is there anything to be learnt from this or not?
6. Which accomplishments would make you feel the most proud of yourself?
7. Which accomplishments will leave behind a legacy, a tangible outcome, a sense of permanence, or can be passed on to someone else who can benefit? This way of thinking might not be helpful for everybody, because it will depend on what your values are. Some people love the idea of producing something that has a sense of permanence, and that can be of value to others even in the absence of their own presence.
8. In ten years from now, how important will this accomplishment be to you? Another great perspective is to use the rocking chair technique. Imagine that you've come to the end of your life and you are reflecting back on your achievements. Which achievements seem the most important from this perspective?

9. Is this particular goal *your actual* goal or is it simply a means or an approach to achieve a greater goal? For instance, a goal might be to run five times a week. Is the real goal the act of running five times per week, or is it simply the means or approach to a higher level goal which is to actually lose ten pounds? If your goal is simply a means, is it the best means towards your goal, or is there another approach?
10. What are your core values, and which goals are most in line with these values? Do you know what your top ten values are? If you haven't done so already, I recommend making a list of these core values. Here's a brief list to get you thinking:

- Financial freedom
- Wealth
- Money
- Prestige
- Ambition
- Health
- Fitness
- Well-being
- Relationships
- Family
- Leisure/Recreation time
- Fun
- Adventure
- Risk-taking
- Learning and Education
- Personal Growth
- Accomplishment
- Achievement
- Career
- Security
- Life Balance
- Compassion
- Happiness and Harmony
- Independence
- Control

If you are looking for more assistance on how to discover your values, I highly recommend that you peruse a few of these comprehensive lists online: http://www.stevepavlina.com/articles/list-of-values.htm, or http://www.timethoughts.com/goalsetting/ListOfSampleValues.htm. You can also try a popular, free online assessment at www.authentichappiness.org. You'll want to complete the Via Signature Strengths Questionnaire, which measures twenty-four of your character strengths or values. Leave enough time, as there are over two hundred questions.

11. Which goals are fully in your control and not dependent on other people? If you consider yourself to be a very independent person and value freedom a lot, then you'll want to carefully consider this question. You'll become very frustrated if you start collaboratively pursuing a goal with another person, team of people, organization, or association, and then they fail to uphold their end of an agreement.

    Sometimes, when you are lacking confidence, you might be tempted to tag team with a friend, a family member, an acquaintance, or a business partner on a goal simply because you think it will make the process easier. For instance, maybe you are thinking of starting a small business or developing a new product or service. However, maybe you believe that you need to rely upon another person's expertise. While this can be helpful, it doesn't mean that you can't run the show on your own. There are many mentors and coaches available to help you pursue your goals. So, if you truly want to pursue your goals independently, go for it. It is a myth to believe that you need to rely on someone else.

12. Is this goal an external "should" or an internal desire?
13. If you could take action in spite of your fear, what might you want for yourself right now?

14. Which goals and their required efforts would best fit into the "flow" or pace of your life? In other words, you don't want to feel as though you are forcing a goal to completion. Which goals fit best within your current life context and/or circumstances? Which goals are easiest or most reasonable to start working towards right now?
15. What *needs* to be done right now? Do any of your goals need your attention or action steps now even though you won't receive a pay-off or results until a much later time?
16. Are there any goals that won't take up much time overall, but are vitally important and can be accomplished in a short time, right away?
17. What have you been meaning to do all your life, but have never found the *right* time to start it? *You probably want to consider embarking on this goal now.*
18. Which goals are purely wishes? For example, which goals are things you'd love to be, do, or have, but only if it came easily to you? Out of the goals that you are considering, can you realistically see yourself following through with the needed action steps or would you lose interest in the goal if you became frustrated along the way?

I can remember at one point in my life feeling a bit frustrated as I wasn't making much progress with a few of the goals that I was pursuing. I had put an ad in the paper to look for a partner for a joint venture to buy real estate. My phone rang off the hook, and I had several meetings with individuals, but I never found the right "fit." Then, I paired up with another individual and we put "no money down" offers on several houses. Unfortunately, our low-ball offers were refused. I became frustrated because I felt as though I was chasing my tail. In retrospect, I understand that I wasn't putting in 100 percent of my effort, because it truly wasn't "me" and it wasn't my number one passion. For some reason, that goal didn't seem to fit with who I was at the time. I felt somewhat detached from these goals the entire time. What

I really wanted to pursue was something that I would have a lot more passion and control over, and could do on my own time, independent of other people. Eventually, I returned to pursuing the development of one of my websites and my personal writing that I wanted to publish. This was something that resonated closer to my core values. Out of the goals that you are considering, which ones resonate closer with your values?

19. Despite natural and inevitable barriers, fears, and temporary setbacks, which goals can you expect yourself to always have a renewed interest in? Can you see any patterns of interest from the past? Which goals do you see yourself persisting with despite these inherent complexities and barriers that you'll face?
20. Perhaps you've focused exclusively on goals pertaining to one area of your life, and you need to balance it out by pursuing goals in other areas of your life. What types of goals would give you this balance?
21. Are there any goals that feel as though your name is "written all over it"? Do you feel an unusual calling towards any of these goals even if you can't logically explain it? Are there any patterns or themes you've experienced throughout your life that suggest that you should tackle a particular goal?

I've certainly experienced an interesting theme in my own life with respect to having an intense passion for reading psychology and personal development books as well as listening to their audio programs. Early on in high school, I remember walking into bookstores and purchasing five to seven books at a time simply because I was so excited to learn success principles that I could apply to my life immediately. When I was in my late teens, I decided that I, too, wanted to write my own personal development book. However, it wasn't until I was older and realized the importance of this goal to me that I finally gave myself the permission to take my goal of writing a book seriously. By this point in time, I was able to recognize the regularity and intensity of this pattern of interest in my life. It really helped to validate and confirm the direction that I was headed in.

22. Which goals might have resulted from purely social influence, pressure, or suggestions from the people around you? Which goals seemed to have developed from within yourself? Which goals stem from your internal passion versus a stance of trying to prove something to yourself or to someone else?

So, did you experience any light bulb moments as you read through the list of questions? Did you notice any patterns of certain goals being seriously considered over and over again? I hope you have a better idea of what you want to focus on now.

Whichever goal you choose, you must have passion, emotion, and a real personal drive behind your goal. A great piece of advice from Steve Pavlina is to "focus your attention on goals that inspire and motivate you right now, since the present moment is the only place you have any real power" (Pavlina, 2009).

A NOTE ON BECOMING FOCUSED

It is a myth to believe that after reading a particular book, attending a particular seminar, or finishing a session with your life coach or counsellor that you will suddenly "discover" or find that one all-empowering, life changing, singular "focus," or life goal that is supposed to change your life in a significant way. The realization of a person's life goals and dreams are most often never decided upon in one single moment, day, week, or even a month. That is not to say that it cannot and does not happen, because it does. We've all had pivotal moments in which we've felt enlightened, been able to make major life decisions, or found a new sense of clarity and direction. My hope is that these questions and exercises at the very least have helped you to identify some of your core values, and simultaneously have helped you narrow down your many passions, so that you can develop a sense of focus. Although we all hope to identify the exact goal that we should focus on now that will transform our life, it is important to note that most of the time, for most people, the reality is that passion and focus develop and evolve over time, through a series of learning experiences, actions, and reflective insights. So, don't be hard on yourself if you still haven't experienced the big "ah-ha" moment or if you haven't pinpointed the exact life path that you should take. Your particular path may not be like that. Be thankful for whatever insights you have gained thus far.

SO, YOU'VE IDENTIFIED YOUR GOAL, BUT NOW WHAT?

Now that you have done some considerable reflection around which goals are most important to you, you are ready to move on to the next set of exercises. In order to benefit the most from the rest of this goal-setting program, I recommend that you begin by choosing one of your top goals to complete the rest of the exercises with.

After you get the hang of how these exercises work, you will want to apply each of these exercises to the rest of your goals. Let the instructions in this book act as a blueprint that can guide you in achieving any goal. After you get practice with these exercises and build your goal-setting muscles, it will become quicker and much easier.

CHAPTER 5

Smart Women Love to Plan!

HOW DO I WRITE DOWN MY GOALS?

> Plan today, to reap the rewards tomorrow!

Many women ask me all the time, "What is the proper way to write down my goals?" Think about what is more important: spending time on the formality of how to turn a goal into a sentence or focusing on taking steps to turn your goal into reality? Too many people get stuck in the minutiae and detail of something that is actually insignificant, compared to other important factors. More important than how we write our goals down are factors such as:

1) Remembering that you actually have goals
2) Planning how you'll achieve your goals
3) Learning how to motivate yourself into action on a *consistent* basis, not just in the beginning.

As you refine your goals over time, and re-write them, and even when you set new goals, you'll want to keep the following few guidelines in mind. Here are some basic tips.

THE VALUE OF THE PRESENT TENSE AND "I" STATEMENTS

It's recommended that you write your goals in the present tense as if you had already achieved them. The rationale is that by using the present tense, you are tricking your brain into believing that you have already achieved that goal. Your brain cannot distinguish the difference between information that is presented in the past or present. When you present your goal statements to yourself in present tense as if they were already coming to fruition, your subconscious is more likely to accept this as reality. This means that your subsequent thoughts and behaviours begin supporting the achievement of that goal.

Finally, whenever possible, use the pronoun "I" when writing down your goals. This creates a sense and feeling of ownership and responsibility for your goals. It also makes your goal seem more real every time you read it. Think of these suggestions as experiential tools that can increase the extent to which your goals feel real. This in turn means more motivation for you.

SMART WOMEN LOVE WRITING ACTION PLANS

There is a well known saying that, the road of someday leads down the path to nowhere. Thus, the point of writing an action plan is to help you focus and to plan "how" your goal will unfold. Why leave your goal to chance? Learn *how* you are going to make it happen.

Here is the easiest and simplest way to get started writing an action plan. Note the description *easiest and simplest*. Your action plans must be simple or you won't get into the habit of using them. Keeping the action plan simple is especially important given that you're already up against a new challenge—achieving a big goal!

PLANNING TO GET STARTED WITH YOUR GOAL!

Often tackling a new goal requires a lot of planning ahead of time just to get started with your goal. Here is a quick way to plan ahead.

1. Write a list of all the potential actions, tasks, or mini-steps that need to be taken to achieve your goal. What you are doing is breaking your goal down into manageable steps. Don't worry about the order of these steps. Just write down everything that you know (thus far) that is involved. Here's an example:

   Goal: I'm in the process of exercising five times per week.

   - Get new exercise clothing and shoes
   - Make an appointment to get orthotics

- Hire a personal trainer
- Find upbeat songs to put on my Mp3 player
- Exercise five times per week, for one hour

2. Prioritize these steps by numbering them in order of what needs to be started or completed first, then second, and so on.

   - Get new exercise clothing and shoes—2
   - Make an appointment to get orthotics—1
   - Hire a personal trainer—3
   - Find upbeat songs to put on my Mp3 player—4
   - Exercise five times per week, for one hour—5

3. Post this list beside your most common work space. Simply choose an action that makes the most sense to get started with it. Schedule a time in your calendar for when you'll complete this action. When you are finished with this action, cross it off your list.
4. Continue to take action, and when you are ready, move onto another item on your list. Schedule this in your calendar as well. At the beginning of each week, review your action plan and determine what your next steps will be for the week. According to Steve Pavlina, a successful leader in personal development, "You don't need crisp deadlines, and you don't need detailed step-by-step plans. You simply need a burning desire to take action" (Pavlina, 2009).

What's more important than how quickly you achieve your goals is that you *don't lose sight* of your goals. As long as we are in the habit of constantly returning our focus to our goals and giving our goals the attention and nurturance that they deserve, we'll make progress. If we continually take steps in the right direction, then we haven't given up at all.

PLANNING YOUR DAILY AND WEEKLY HABITS

In the above example, the action plan was all about the preparation that was needed, in order for me to get my goal started. However, there's more to it, because I needed to plan out my habits as well. Here's what you need to do:

1. Write a list of all the habits required on a daily and weekly basis to maintain the goal of working out five times per week. For example:

    - Make sure workout clothes are packed in a bag the night before
    - Make sure I buy healthy groceries every Sunday morning
    - Ensure I have afternoon snacks available at work before I leave for my workout
    - Plan workouts for the week

2. These habits must occur simultaneously, but the trick is planning a time in your calendar in which you can regularly commit to these habits.

    - Make sure workout clothes are packed for the next day—pack clothes just before bedtime
    - Make sure I buy healthy groceries every week—Sunday mornings before I do anything else
    - Ensure I have an afternoon snack available at work before I leave to my workout—pack the night before
    - Plan workouts for the week—plan this Friday morning

For these habits, I recommend creating a check-list of these habits and posting them somewhere, so that you can see them every day to remind yourself to execute them. We need constant reminders of the things that we want to get done every day. Advertisers are good at persuading people into action, because they understand the power of repetition and visual reminders.

Take advantage of this technique, and use your check-list as an advertisement to keep yourself in action with your habits.

You'll want to advertise these steps in your calendar as well, as a reminder to make sure you complete them. For instance, on Sunday, write "buy groceries." Remember, in advertising, the most effective way to persuade people to take action and buy their products is through constant repetition of their messages. So, post your list of steps and keep them visible.

ACTION PLANNING WITH DEADLINES

The point of using a deadline is not only to ensure that the goal is achieved by a certain date, but it is also to provide motivation. A deadline is a guideline only, and it forces you to start with the end in mind. Deadlines might drive you nuts, but you know they will provide you with the necessary motivation you're looking for. If this is the case, try using deadlines to your advantage.

1. Choose a final deadline or date by which you'd like to complete your entire goal.
2. Write a list of all the action steps or tasks that might be required for you to achieve your goal. This is a way of "chunking" things down.
3. Review each of these action steps and decide upon the most effective order in which to complete these steps. Write a 1 beside the step that you want to work on first. Then, write a 2 beside the next most important step, and so on.
4. Beside each step, you can write down a specific date by which you plan to complete this particular action step.

MISSED DEADLINES AND LEARNING OPPORTUNITIES

Remember that you always need to be flexible with the dates and the order that you attach to your action plan and its steps. With each action or step that you take towards your goal, you will learn new information, find new resources, and discover things you didn't even know that you didn't know. As a result, you will constantly be re-evaluating and changing your plan to some extent. You must be open-minded to integrate the new information you discover as you move towards the completion of your goals.

Also, even when you have plans in place, unexpected things can come up in your schedule. Often, we'll know about them in advance. Get into the habit of reviewing each week ahead of time and planning your schedule accordingly, so you can commit to the necessary tasks for the week.

Of course, even when you do use deadlines, there are going to be many times when you don't actually achieve your goal by that date. You can learn a lot about yourself and your work style when you miss a deadline. Review some of the possible reasons. Was the pace of your work or the frequency of your action steps too stressful and overwhelming? Did your schedule not allow for more flexibility or freedom to attend to other things? Did you lack time, and if so, why? Did you not find a good routine or schedule that was comfortable for you to stick to? Whenever you find yourself not making as much progress as you'd like, pause and reflect on what is standing in your way. Some of the best learning lessons in life are from the mistakes and errors that we make along the way.

More important than how much you have perfected the "plan" with schedules and deadlines is how often you are taking action with the steps that you have written down. As long as you are taking consistent action, you will eventually get to where you want to go. One amazing technique that you can begin using right away is visualization. It will keep you inspired, hopeful, energized, and it is a great way to restate and reinforce the goals that you want to achieve.

USE THE POWER OF VISUALIZATION

Perhaps one of the most important reasons to write your goals down is so that you are constantly flooded with images of yourself achieving your goals. As I mentioned in the first chapter, the brain exercises itself through the use of images and words that we continually can read by "seeing" them.

By visualizing your goals, many things begin to happen. Seeing an image is very experiential, so it makes it easy for you to imagine and experience your goal in the *present* tense—*now*. Seeing a picture of your goal makes it easier to believe in your big goal, simply because of how real it feels. Also, the actual image of your desired goal can easily *ignite your emotion*.

If you can visualize your goals, collect images, pictures, or any visual reminder of your goal, then you will begin to trick your subconscious mind into believing that these goals are already a part of your reality, or that they are in the process of becoming your reality.

Visualization doesn't need to be complicated. You don't need to hypnotize yourself or sit down and meditate for hours on end. Many people, including myself, find it too tedious to do the traditional imaginative exercises in our heads. I know this has been one of the most difficult exercises for many of the clients I've worked with. We lose concentration, we fall asleep, or for some other reason, it just doesn't appeal to us. We haven't trained our minds to work well on that level.

Any written goals, verbal messages or images presented over and over again to yourself will eventually be accepted by your subconscious mind as reality. The more this happens, the more your brain will go to work to close the gap between your current reality and what continues to be suggested. This is how advertising works. After you read or hear about a message often enough, your brain begins to "buy into" that message, and then you unconsciously begin to act as though you *need* that product. As a result, you take action and decide to buy the advertised product.

Learn to apply the same concepts from marketing and advertising to the achievement of your own life goals. Read your goals often, because repetition and constant reminders are the key. Also, the more you read your goals in present tense, the more you believe that they are actually happening.

So, here are some great ways to speed up the process of achieving your goals by using the power of visualization.

EASY AND EFFECTIVE WAYS TO VISUALIZE YOUR GOALS

1. Print off a nicely organized list of your goals or action steps for a particular goal, and then insert this list into a nice picture frame. Place this frame somewhere that you will see it every single day. Rather than having your goals written on some piece of paper or notebook shoved in a drawer, now you have them on display. You can get as obsessed as you want with this technique. You might have several different frames up, each entailing a list of action steps for your various goal projects. Or you might have several frames up, each frame listing a different category of life goals.
2. Buy a really attractive or appealing greeting card from your local store. Inside the card, write out all your goals, or one goal and the action steps for this particular goal. You might even want to include a picture of you along with your achieved goal. Keep this card sitting on your bedside table, your desk, or even posted on your fridge, wall, or bulletin board. Whenever you have a spare minute, read through your goals and action steps. Alternatively, you could also review these goals each morning and/or each night. By writing your goals and action steps in a beautiful card, it ensures that you don't shove the card in a drawer where it will get lost. Because you've written your goals down on something that you paid several dollars for, you are more likely to keep that card in an easily accessible, visible location.

3. Use technology to your advantage. Write your goals and respective actions onto your computer screen saver or regular desktop background. How's that for a constant visualization reminder? Remember, repetition is the key to your success. Another idea is to try programming one of your big goals onto the face-top of your cell phone.
4. Instead of displaying your driver's license picture in your wallet, try using that visual space to insert a printed version or a picture of what is most important for you to focus on completing right now. You might even put a motivational quote or reminder in there.
5. Use sticky notes to write down all the action steps needed for one of your current goals. Post it right beside your desk where you work most often. This way, whenever you encounter a lull in motivation or a barrier, you will constantly be reminded of the steps that you need to execute to continue with your goal. Another alternative is to write each task on a separate note and take down the note once you've completed the task or goal.

Often, when people run into barriers with their goals, they become foggy-minded, fooled, and disillusioned about the reality of what is happening. Soon, their fear and negative emotions paralyze them. They forget what they need to do or try next to get started again. Don't let the bumps in the road cause you to forget what to try next. Have this note of action steps on your wall, so you always have a visual to remind you of what you need to do.

7. Use the power of email. Email yourself and in the subject title, simply write an action step or goal. Don't delete this email until you have completed the action or achieved the goal. Every time you log in to your email, you will be reminded of your goals or action steps.
8. Create a vision board. Buy a bulletin board and hang it somewhere visible. Then, cut out the pictures that symbolize your goals and all that you want to do, be, and have in your

life. You can even post real pictures of you that show you achieving your goals. Keep on the look-out for inspirational pictures in magazines, newspapers, etc. Clip them out and post them on your board.

9. Use a whiteboard and create mind-maps. Using dry erase markers that are easily wiped off, you can create a mind-map by drawing circles that represent how all your ideas or action steps are connected. This provides a good visual strategy when you're not quite sure how the order of all your steps will unfold. Alternatively, write your to-do list on your whiteboard for the day, week, or month. Organize it however you want, but keep it somewhere you can see every single day.
10. Use a scrapbook. If you want a more private medium, then you can store all your visuals in a book. However, keep this book right by your bedside table. In the morning and/or evening, pull out your scrapbook, and flip through all your goal lists, pictures, and other inserts as reminders.
11. Buy a spiral-bound journal with a hardcover—one that is really beautiful with nice designs on the pages. Buy a nice book or picture stand, and place your journal on it, with the journal opened to the pages that list your goals. As your goals or to-do lists change, simply turn the page, update your list, and put it back on your display stand. I love this one, and I keep mine sitting right on my desk by my computer monitor.
12. Read through *all* lists of your goals as frequently as you can. Some people read their goals every day. For others, once a week is plenty. Get in the habit of re-visiting your goals, so that you stay focused and don't forget about them.

So, now you have a good handful of techniques that will help you visualize your goals. These are practical and tangible strategies that are guaranteed to boost your productivity, keep you focused, and give you all the benefits of traditional visualization.

POWER QUESTIONS—USING VISUALIZATION TO SUPPORT YOUR GOALS

1. What other visual symbols or tangible items could you put in your environment to remind you of your goals and required action steps?
2. What visual strategies have motivated you or kept you focused on your goals in the past?
3. What do you have the most difficulty imagining or "seeing" in terms of your success? How can you find a real visible snapshot of this?

CHAPTER 6

Why Is It So Difficult to Achieve BIG Goals?

CHANGE IS THE REAL CHALLENGE

> Those who expect moments of change to be comfortable and free of conflict have not learned their history.
> -Joan Wallach Scott

All right, you've set your goal and you have a plan of action. Have you ever come this far in the past, but then not followed through on your action plan? Does this sound familiar?

Perhaps you're someone who has read all the self-help books, listened to all the audio programs, and attended all the motivational seminars on personal growth, but you're still not achieving the results you want in your life. In fact, maybe you've even skipped over this goal-setting section because you've already completed exercises like these a million times. You're thinking, *I've already done this goal-setting stuff and it's gotten me nowhere.*

The truth is that goal setting alone does not guarantee anything, because it is only one tiny part of the success formula. You might have set goals time and time again, but constantly found yourself wondering why you don't *do* what you *say* you're going to do. There is lots of excitement in the beginning when we start accomplishing a few of the tasks on our list, but we can suddenly get sidetracked, or even worse, forget that we had a plan to stick to in the first place.

Sometimes, we desire our goal so intensely, but then, no matter what efforts and hard work we put forth, we feel as though we're trying to run through neck-deep water, but we can't get anywhere fast enough. It's not uncommon for people to get angry or frustrated with themselves for not following through with their plans or being disciplined enough.

At times, we can be disciplined with our action steps, but we observe barriers that get in our way. Then, we explain the reasons we never accomplished what we wanted. In fact, I'm sure we all have stories behind each goal that we weren't able to accomplish.

The challenge doesn't stop in your goal setting and knowing what you want in life. The real challenge is self-management—being able to activate your personal power, take action, and follow through with your goals no matter what. Think about it. How would your life be different if you knew with absolute certainty that you could get yourself to follow through with your goals and action plans?

Imagine what kind of momentum your life would have if your actions were aligned with your intentions. What if you could guarantee that whatever goals you set, they would become your reality?

The first part of this book was about helping you to dream big, prioritize your dreams, and then get focused on your most important goals. The rest of this book is going to address the challenge of making sure that you motivate yourself and change any limiting beliefs and habits that may stand in your way. I am going to show you self-motivation techniques based on scientific research, so that you can motivate yourself no matter where you are in the process of achieving your goals.

WHY IS IT SO DIFFICULT TO ACHIEVE OUR GOALS?

So, why is achieving our goals so difficult at times? The achievement of goals boils down to the accumulation and execution of excellent habits. These habits can be recurring thoughts, feelings, behaviours, and actions. Therefore, to achieve an important goal, we must make *changes* to our habits of thinking, feeling, and acting. This is the reason achieving our goals can seem so difficult. Trying to change our habits is difficult, because it requires continual effort and persistence. A lot of effort must be invested in the beginning with few immediate payoffs. Seldom is there immediate gratification when forming a new habit.

FALSE PROMISES OF CHANGE IN THE MEDIA

I'm sure you've heard of the following promises or advertisements—a personal change program that promises you riches in less than a few months, or programs that guarantee you'll lose thirty pounds in thirty days and keep it off for good. So many programs focus exclusively on getting people into *action* immediately. People want to change and achieve their goals quickly, so the first thing they do is take *action.* Have you ever noticed how most people's New Year's resolutions often fail? It is because they rushed into taking the necessary actions, but they skipped the necessary steps of preparation and planning. The problem, however, is that they haven't done any long-term planning to change their mindsets and behaviours, so they fail or give up.

On the converse, sometimes people will say, *I know what to do, but I'm just not doing it!* In other words, they can't get motivated to take any action. Maybe you know that you need to start saving more money, spending more time with your partner, or taking better care of yourself. But knowing the needed habits and actions required isn't enough if you can't motivate yourself.

I believe that to successfully achieve your goals and to make important life changes, it is really helpful to have an awareness of how your mind operates in relation to change and achievement. Do you truly understand the process involved in achieving your goals? Once you become aware of the steps to success and the necessary changes involved, you can monitor your progress and gain control of your life. This is a tool you'll have forever.

Achieving your goals and doing "change work" involves so much more than taking action. The key is to plan for how you'll overcome all the challenges along the way.

THE SCIENCE OF PERSONAL CHANGE

There is a large body of research that exists on how to make changes to our habits and behaviours. My aim is to apply several of these change principles and stages to the topic of goal setting.

The research and application of the "Stages of Change" Model (Prochaska, Norcross, & Diclemente, 1994) has been successful in helping people to make certain behavioural changes, including quitting smoking, drinking and problem gambling, losing weight, finding a job, improving moods, and becoming more social. It has also been effective in treating various interpersonal or psychological challenges, including depression, anxiety, and many other ailments. The six stages of change that have been scientifically proven to help people change and quit bad habits include precontemplation, contemplation, preparation, action, maintenance, and termination.

PERSONAL CHANGE AND GOAL-SETTING ACHIEVEMENT

The Stages of Change Model has strong applications in helping people to quit behaviours and ameliorate various psychological difficulties. However, there is a lot of value in building on this change model and applying this knowledge to the stages of goal-setting achievement, which also involves overcoming barriers, solving problems, and changing beliefs and behaviours. What's different in goal-setting achievement is that when people set goals, they are usually striving to self-actualize and meet higher order needs, along with fulfilling their dreams, desires, and wants in general. Making changes to achieve a goal as opposed to eradicating a behaviour or psychological ailment also requires a certain degree of "stick-to-it-ness." Whether we're trying to accomplish a higher order need or desire, or quit a dysfunctional behaviour, such as a gambling addiction, we are striving to solve problems that prevent us from achieving our goal. In order to achieve our goals, we must make changes to our skill sets, mindsets, and habits, in order to consistently execute the necessary actions needed to achieve our goals.

Within each stage of change are tasks that an individual must address or work through in order to achieve her goals. Tasks might include adopting certain mindsets, attitudes, coping skills, or behaviours. There are critical learning principles and lessons to be digested at each stage, along with important tasks that are crucial to helping people achieve *any* important life goal.

In the Stage of Change Model, there is the general notion that completion of each stage is incremental, meaning that completing the tasks in one stage provides a solid foundation for moving onto the next stage, and so forth. Of course, it is noted that change is never linear. No one perfectly progresses in a straightforward manner without regressing. Also, a person can be working through several different "stages" at a time, addressing the necessary tasks as needed.

> *Nobody can go back and start a new beginning,*
> *but anyone can start today and make a new ending.*
> *-Maria Robinson*

Inherent within the stages of change are many valuable principles to help you achieve your life goals. I have borrowed from and expanded upon this research by applying it specifically to what I refer to as the stages of goal-setting achievement. Thus, from this point on, I will be referring to the stages of goal-setting achievement. Likewise, I will discuss the corresponding tasks of goal achievement that are necessary at each stage.

STAGES OF GOAL-SETTING ACHIEVEMENT

In the first stage of goal-setting achievement, which I refer to as the *acknowledgment of the present,* individuals are in a state of denial, and not fully aware that they want to strive for something more with respect to their goals. A person has numbed herself to her desire to achieve her goal. She is out of touch with how discomforting and psychologically painful it is to remain in her current situation. To move through this goal-setting stage, she must perceive the negatives of her current situation to outweigh the positives. Once this happens, she is more likely to start committing to her goals and the necessary changes that achieving her goals will require. We'll be addressing the tasks of this goal-setting stage in the next chapter.

During the second stage of goal-setting achievement, *commitment to the future,* a person must confront the issue of how committed she is to her goal. To do this, she must perceive the benefits of achieving her goal as being greater than the perceived negative factors and fears of achieving her goal. In other words, the advantages of committing to her goals must outweigh the disadvantages. When this occurs, she is much more ready and serious to begin the real work of striving towards her goal. You will complete these tasks in chapter eight.

The third stage of goal-setting achievement, *preparation,* involves experimenting with actions, while also getting ready to address barriers. In the stages of goal-setting achievement, this involves addressing one's limiting belief systems and substituting healthy beliefs. It also involves identifying limiting behaviours and planning substitutions for these limiting behaviours. Achieving goals requires a lot of planning, and you'll be completing tasks that will assist you with this in chapters nine, ten, and eleven.

The fourth stage of goal-setting achievement, *momentum*, marks the point at which a person is fully engaged and committed to the new mindsets, habits, and actions that are necessary to achieve and maintain her goals. The fifth stage of goal setting achievement is *engagement,* which involves continual execution of the new habits and behaviours over the long term.

Finally, the last stage of goal-setting achievement is *automaticity*. At this point, an individual no longer has to exert effort or pay much attention to her achievements. In other words, her changes and new accomplishments feel automatic, and there is no sense of ever slipping back to her old ways. More than anything, this is often an ideal. However, it is always worth striving for. The truth is, however, that to maintain and achieve our goals will always require a constant investment of our time, efforts, and energy. While this is the case, eventually, a person can reach a point where her investment of time and effort *seems* effortless and her results are achieved with greater ease.

The following cited research on the Stages of Goal-setting Achievement is drawn from the original Stages of Change Model and then expanded further and tailored specifically to the context of goal setting. There is no need to try to reinvent your own wheel of change and achievement. There is already a science behind the following stages and corresponding tasks suggested within this book. If you can complete the following exercises and return to them over time as needed, you will increase the speed and ease with which you can achieve your big goals.

Achieving your goals and making the necessary life changes is not easy. It requires work, planning, preparation, and a lot of action. But it *is* possible if you follow the key principles that many successful people have already used, whether or not they realized it at the time. The next section of this book gives you that process.

CHAPTER 7

Acknowledgment of the Present

YOUR CURRENT SITUATION: IS IT WORTH STAYING?

When was the last time you had a really good look in the mirror to catch a glimpse of what your current situation with your life goals is like? For some of us, this may not sound like a fun exercise, but there is a lot of value behind acknowledging your current situation. This is important because, in order to embrace our future goals, we need to get un-stuck from our current situation. People remain in their current situation, because they are comfortable. In other words, your current situation is likely your comfort zone. But is your comfort zone worth staying in? This is a task worth figuring out. In order to make the necessary changes to achieve your goals, you must be able to acknowledge, come to terms with, or accept your present situation, because it *is* your reality at this point in time. By gaining awareness into the reasons you stay in your current situation, it will be easier to move past it and to commit to your future goals.

In the Stages of Change Model, the first stage of change is referred to as *precontemplation* (Prochaska, Norcross, & Diclemente, 1994). Think of this term just as it reads: *pre* and *contemplate*. When a person isn't contemplating or considering making any changes at all, it's almost as if she has her "blinders" on. She is essentially described as being stuck. These same principles apply to the first stage of goal-setting achievement, *acknowledgment of the present*. This is when a person isn't considering making changes or taking action to move towards her goals at all. For example, if a person is grossly in debt, she isn't acknowledging the problem of her debt, nor is she planning on getting out of debt. I can bet you that deep down inside, she is feeling badly about her debt. If a person is in an unhealthy relationship, she might ignore the fact altogether and remain in denial. This doesn't mean she doesn't feel badly about being in the relationship. At this stage, people are often described as being in denial. Throughout your efforts to achieve your various life goals, you may find yourself unconsciously reverting back to this stage. What does this mean?

Maybe you've tried several times to open a business, but it failed each time. Perhaps you've applied all the self-help advice in your relationships, but each of your relationships failed. With each failure, many people naturally lose hope. You begin to assume that you already know everything there is to know about achieving your goal, but what you know just doesn't work. Therefore, you assume that *nothing works.* You've tried it all, and you feel like a failure. You begin to give up, and resist change altogether to protect yourself from further embarrassment and shame. Let's face it, it's always safest and more comfortable to put on our "blinders" and ignore our problems and woes.

If you're the type of person who is constantly striving to achieve your life goals, then you know what it's like to experience a lot of disappointment along the way. Thus, it might be easy for you to give up and revert back to living in your current situation where you are stuck. For example, you can become sick and tired of investing your money and time into various pursuits to help you reach your goals. You might feel silly, naïve, or disillusioned for confidently believing in your dreams and putting forth the necessary efforts and actions. You might look back and resent the amount of money you invested in new books, audio programs, online courses and products, seminars, and so forth that you thought would help you become closer to your goals. Perhaps you even hired a personal life coach, which is quite common these days. But after a lot of effort and very little pay off to you, it can all feel like a waste of money. There may be a lot of regret and an overwhelming sense of loss. In addition, you might also resent the amount of time that seems to have been "lost." Perhaps you sacrificed a lot of time away from your friends and family, so that you could partake in the necessary research, learning, and personal development that you thought was needed to achieve your goals. Then, you might wonder, *what was it all for?*

After these types of experiences, it is no wonder that you may have little confidence or self-efficacy in your ability to achieve your goals. You might even feel like you have so little control, because everything you tried to achieve your goals failed in the end. Can you relate to this? You might literally have no motivation to work towards your goal when you're in this stage, because you feel hopeless, and you begin to doubt if you could ever really make the necessary changes or execute the appropriate actions to achieve your goals. Or you might be hurt, resentful, and holding onto negative feelings, because none of your efforts have panned out.

JUSTIFYING YOUR CURRENT SITUATION

What can often happen is that a person begins to justify her current situation. For instance, a person is broke, but *that's just the way life is.* Or maybe a person smokes a pack of cigarettes a day, but hey—*you only live life once.* When you are exercising this mindset, you might end up excusing yourself from taking responsibility for your life goals. When you do this, you are in denial of what's truly important, and you feel safe, because you don't need to confront anything that's holding you back. Allowing fear or doubt to paralyze you is a way of staying safe, because you maintain complete control and are able to avoid failure and threats. You have total freedom from trying to compete with the world to achieve your goals.

You might also begin to tell yourself that your goal is unrealistic, or that it's not important. You act disinterested, sarcastic, or resentful if others are discussing the topic, e.g., making more money or achieving better life balance than you are. You might even feel resentful of those who have successfully achieved the goals that *you* want. You might blame your external environment for your lack of success and your inability to take the important steps or make the necessary changes.

After truly believing that your goal is not possible to achieve, or that it's too hard to make the necessary changes required, you bury yourself further in denial and solidify the belief that attaining your goal isn't even possible. Then, what happens is that you don't even pay attention to anything that could possibly help you achieve your goals. When your blinders are on, you don't notice the new resources, key contact persons, or great opportunities. In other words, you minimize or soon forget about your goal and your true desires for the future. You become wrapped up in the day-to-day hustle and bustle of life. You might know deep down that you wish you could take the necessary steps to achieve your goal, but very rarely does this desire ever come to the forefront of your mind. When you're in this stage, you've basically set your goals and dreams aside. This doesn't sound like a good place to be, does it?

THE TURNING POINT

Obviously, there is good news. Eventually, of course, there is a turning point, and you move forward. What often happens is a person begins to recognize the risks of being complacent with her current life. Similarly, she might experience a spark of awareness that life could be better. Usually, a person becomes really frustrated or dissatisfied with her current life or particular situation.

What might push a person to break out of her settlement mentality is pain, which has been thought to be one of our greatest motivators. In order to increase your self-motivation and move towards your goals, it is crucial that you become very aware of the negative consequences of *not* achieving your goal. The risks of remaining in your current situation should outweigh the positive rewards of your current situation. When this change in awareness and mindset occurs, you will want to take action and make the necessary changes that will move you closer to your goal.

It's important to use emotional arousal to your benefit and to focus on the negative aspects of what it is you want to move away from. For example, if you want to make a career change, it is wise to write a list of the negative consequences you'll experience if you don't make that career change. How will your life be worse off? How will your personal development suffer if you don't take the necessary steps? If you want to move away from being broke, then imagine the negative consequences of what your life will be like if you continue to overspend.

The key is to attach negative thoughts to the specific elements of your current situation that you are hoping to move away from. If your goal involves moving away from a bad habit or problem, such as overeating or overspending, you might not feel motivated to take action, because you are numb to the negative consequences and not experiencing them intensely enough. Therefore, it might help to really focus on the long-term negative consequences of your behaviour, *in addition* to your current negative consequences that you are experiencing. This isn't about beating yourself up. Rather, it's about developing an awareness of why you want to move away from your current situation.

WHAT ARE THE BENEFITS OF YOUR CURRENT SITUATION?

In addition to coming to terms with what bothers you about your current situation, it is also important to understand how you are benefitting from your current situation or lifestyle. I encourage people to examine both the pros and cons of their current situation. The table below provides a visual overview of how your aim is to become aware of what's positive and negative in your current situation (in which you have not achieved your goal).

Your Current Situation

What's Negative?

- What are the negative consequences?
- What is painful?
- What are the immediate and long-term risks of staying how you are?
- The "dis-comfort zone" reveals the "dangers" in staying here.
- Focusing on this motivates you to move away from your current state.

What's Positive?

- What are the positive and immediate rewards for remaining here?
- What are the benefits?
- What's pleasurable and joyful?
- Also known as the comfort zone.
- Too much focus/awareness here holds you back.
- Focusing too much on this keeps you stuck in your current situation.

Next, you are going to take an inventory of the negative and positive feelings and thoughts that you have about your current situation. Remember, your current situation is what you are trying to move away from, so that you can accomplish your goal.

Remember that remaining in your present situation has both its pay-offs and costs. Your goal is to become aware of both sides of this equation. You want to create a radical change in your awareness, so that any positive benefits you experience from not being committed to your goal is offset by the negative consequences of not being committed to your goal. You want the *discomfort* of the present to be more intense than the *comfort* of your present, so that you are motivated to take action.

Building an awareness of how you are dissatisfied with your present situation, while also appreciating how you receive pleasure from your present situation, will lead you to personal breakthroughs in how you view your current reality. You will no longer be strongly attached to remaining at your current level of achievement. Instead, you'll be able to let go of what's familiar and move forward with your goals. By developing personal awareness through the following exercises, you will be adopting a new perspective on your current situation, which will help release you from the many attachments to your current situation. Rather than clinging to your present reality that obviously isn't getting you where you want to be, you will experience radical changes in your perspectives that will shift you into fast gear, achieving your goals with much more ease.

Are you ready to experience a radical shift in perspective of your current reality or lifestyle? Turn the page . . .

WHAT'S NEGATIVE ABOUT YOUR CURRENT SITUATION?

Have you ever heard of the notion of the power of negative thinking? I can't remember where I first came across this idea, however, my first reaction was that it was bonkers! How could thinking negative ever be to my advantage? When it comes to achieving your goals, there are some key advantages to "negative thinking."

For instance, what discomfort will you have to face in your life if you don't achieve your goal? What bad feelings will you continue to have about where you are right now? In order to move away from your current situation, it's important to think negatively about remaining in your current situation. What do I mean by focusing on the "negatives" of your current situation? Here are some other pieces of language to keep in mind:

- Discomforts
- The "cons"
- Sense of psychological "pain"
- Frustrations
- Irritations
- Regrets
- Dissatisfactions
- Annoyances
- Depressing aspects
- What's not working
- Negative consequences
- Disadvantages

This exercise is a classic one that has been around for a long time, because it works on manipulating your perception of pleasure versus pain. Anthony Robbins popularized this concept and summarized it nicely by saying that individuals will do much more to move away from pain than they will ever do to move towards pleasure (Robbins, 1991). Think about it. A classic example involves New Year's resolutions. So many people are motivated to set their goals at this time, and when you hear them talk about it, they are always focused on the negative aspects of what they are trying to move away from. For example, people will say they've hit rock bottom by over-spending, over-eating, or giving away too much time to work-related activities and other people. These people are motivated to make changes, based on the negativity they were experiencing.

DRAMATIC REASONS = LEVERAGE

This exercise is helpful in that it helps to gather the reasons on why it would be so awful to *not* achieve your goal. What would your life be like if you knew that you would never achieve this goal?

The more dramatic reasons you can think of, the more compelled you will be to ensure that you do achieve your goals. So, it's time to put on your pessimistic hat and think "negatively" about what you're trying to leave behind in your life. Now, you can understand how negative thinking has its role in success and achievement. Recognize how you will be dissatisfied if you don't achieve this goal. The more negativity you can accumulate here, the more leverage you will have to achieve your goals.

POWER QUESTIONS: WHAT'S NEGATIVE ABOUT MY CURRENT SITUATION?

I have provided you below with a list of power questions that will assist you in identifying the negative consequences of remaining in your current situation. By realizing how "bad" or unfortunate your present reality is without the attainment of your goal, you will increase your motivation.

Some of these questions might seem overly dramatic, but hey, if you want your goal badly enough, you'll play whatever "mind games" are necessary to get yourself into action. Are you willing to do whatever it takes and experiment with this? Are you willing to think in transformative ways? This exercise isn't about feeling good. Rather, its purpose is to quite literally get you in tune with how your current situation is less than favourable, compared to what it could be if you get yourself into action.

1. What kind of knowledge can you gather that will make your situation seem more awful or unpleasant? For example, if your goal is to save money for your retirement, then you might want to run several calculations on what your financial future will look like if you *don't* save any money at all. Do your research and find out how much money you'll need to comfortably maintain the same lifestyle that you have now, but in your retirement. If your goal is to expand and improve the number of relationships in your life, then maybe you'd think about the negative effects of social isolation and not connecting or receiving social support from your network of family and friends. If you are trying to cut caffeine out of your diet, it would be wise for you to know about the dangers of caffeine. Becoming aware of its negative consequences to you is one way of motivating yourself to create a sense of urgency to stop consuming caffeine. If your goal is to cut out sugar from your diet, then you might decide to read a book on the dangers of sugar consumption. Be creative!
2. What are both the short—*and* long-term negative consequences you will experience if you don't achieve your goal? Let's say that your goal is to spend more time with your family and less time on work-related tasks. Your short-term list of things that you are missing out on might include helping your child or teenager with homework, celebrating small victories, such as their success on an assignment or test, or simply enjoying a fun day or weekend with him or her. If you only focus on the short-term sacrifices, it might not seem so bad. However, what happens if you consider the long-term sacrifices? What will the negative consequences be? You might note that your child will have grown apart from you. Or perhaps you never develop that adult-like friendship with your child. Maybe he

or she won't be there for you to celebrate important events in your life. Finally, will your child be around to give you the needed social and/or financial support when you are older? As you can see, sometimes a long-term outlook can be even more motivating than a short-term outlook.

3. What is so comfortable about a comfort zone that will stay the same forever, and that has no real luxuries? What is so fulfilling about living a mediocre lifestyle? How can you think about your current situation or comfort zone as a *danger* zone? What could be potentially risky or dangerous if you remain in your current circumstances right now and don't take any action?
4. What is inconvenient about your current situation or comfort zone? What hassles does it create for you?
5. How does remaining where you are with your current attitudes, emotions, and behaviours affect others negatively?
6. What feelings are present when you remind yourself that you haven't achieved your goal? What disappointment or unpleasant emotions will you struggle with forever if you don't give yourself permission to achieve this goal?
7. For example, Sharon ran a very lucrative business selling flowers and crafts. While she made a lot of money throughout her career, she never seemed to have much time for her family and friends. One of her goals was to take her parents on a vacation, because they were in their retirement and they had very little money. She also wanted to spend some good quality time with them, as she knew that they were getting older and soon might not be able to travel comfortably. Finally, when Sharon was able to get in touch with these feelings, she realized how awful she would feel if she didn't make this a priority. Within a matter of weeks, she had a trip booked with her parents to go on a cruise in the Bahamas.
8. How does remaining in your current lifestyle keep you part of the status quo? In what way is your current comfort zone *too* boring, *too* predictable, or *too* much a part of the status quo? (I'm assuming you don't want to be just like the masses.

Otherwise, you wouldn't be trying so hard to improve your life.)

9. In what way are you living by low standards if you don't become committed to your goal?
10. How will your situation get worse if you don't commit to this goal? This is a really great question to ask yourself if you are seriously working on your health and fitness habits, particularly if you are trying to lose body fat. How will things get worse for you if you don't take control of your weight immediately? With each pound of fat you gain, your weight loss goals will become more difficult. Consider other goals also. How does postponing the achievement of your goal make your situation worse? Also, many people find that delaying their weight loss goals creates a vicious cycle. For example, I once had a client who gained a considerable amount of weight. She began to feel so self-conscious about her weight that she stopped attending her regular social functions with her friends. She even stopped going to the gym to exercise, because she didn't feel good about herself. Then, out of social isolation, she became depressed and ate more food to ameliorate her depression. It was a vicious cycle that was strengthened the longer she delayed making an action plan.
11. What is frustrating about not being 100 percent committed to the path of achieving your goal? How do you feel waking up each morning, knowing that you haven't been committed to your goal?
12. Think of someone you know who had really big dreams and goals, but at some point down the road gave them up and lost commitment for whatever reason. Can you see how dissatisfying her situation and life were as a result? How does this person feel and act on a daily basis now? Do you see how she is missing out on the juice of life? Now the question you need to ask yourself is: *How do I feel about myself when I think of living my life this way? Do I want to live my life this way?*
13. If you don't achieve this goal, how will it prevent you from achieving the other goals in your life?

14. Think carefully about where you stand right now in relation to your goal. What is the worst part about it? Blow it out of proportion. Think of more reasons it is disturbing.
15. What "peer group" are you stuck with as a result of not having achieved your goal? How do you feel being surrounded by people who don't facilitate the achievement of your goal? Would you prefer to mingle with individuals who are on a more similar path to the one you want to be on?
16. Without being committed to the path of achieving your goal, how much are you wasting your potential? What time are you losing? How do you feel when you are *not* embracing your potential?
17. In what ways are you not able to be a role model or positive influence to your family, friends, and desired peer group, as a result of avoiding your goal? Do you smoke, drink, or gamble excessively? What message are you sending to your children? Does anyone avoid you as a result of your bad habits?
18. How can you be comfortable, knowing that others around you, but not yourself, are going from good and better to best in areas of life that are very important to you? How negative does this make you feel?
19. What comforts will you miss out on forever simply because you will not temporarily get yourself out of your comfort zone?
20. How are you devaluing yourself or doing yourself a disservice by failing to take the necessary actions to increase the value of yourself or your self-worth? When you're not on the path to achieving your goal, how is your self-esteem affected negatively?

How did it go? I hope these last few exercises helped you create a sense of urgency for why you *must* change or achieve your goal. Hopefully, you've found a handful of new motivational perspectives in which your current comfort zone is now perceived more as a "disastrous danger zone" that you should move away from. How's that for a piece of motivation? I hope you've gained further reasons to get yourself motivated to do whatever it takes to move forward with your goal. If not, don't worry. There are more exercises coming.

UP NEXT . . .

Next, you are going to examine your current situation, but instead of examining what is negative, you will examine how it is positive, or how it benefits you. In other words, you will gain clarity on how your current situation is a comfort zone. You will understand which of your needs are being fulfilled and met by remaining in a sluggish state of "inaction." Having this awareness will enable you to find other ways to meet these needs and/or comforts.

POSITIVE CONSEQUENCES OF YOUR CURRENT SITUATION

What is so great about remaining in your current situation, also known as your comfort zone, and not having to work towards your goals? How do you benefit? What are the positive consequences of remaining in your current situation? For example, if your goal is to start creating more work-life balance, but you rarely make the effort, then you would need to examine what *is* so great about being so busy all the time.

There are many different ways to think about the positive consequences of your current situation. Here are some alternative pieces of language to help you gain clarity on this concept:

- Benefits
- Positive consequences
- The "pay-offs"
- The "pro's"
- Advantages
- Rewards
- Comforts
- Convenience
- What is positive
- What is safe
- What makes it pleasurable and enjoyable

The next step is to record all the positive consequences of *not* having to be committed to your goal, or of *not* achieving your goal. Read the following list of questions and jot down your answers as you go along. Ready?

POWER QUESTIONS

1. What positive consequences are involved when you don't have to be committed to your goal? What are the positive feelings associated with this present state of comfort?

2. What makes your current situation or "comfort zone" comfortable? How are your needs and values being fulfilled by remaining where you are?
3. How does remaining in your current situation keep you connected to your peers or family group? For instance, do you fear that by taking action towards your goals and being disciplined you will have less time with your friends and family? Do you fear that working towards your goals will isolate you from people in any way?
4. What is enjoyable or convenient about keeping yourself distracted with everything *but* your important life goals? For example, how do you benefit from keeping busy all of the time? Does it allow you the pleasure of avoiding something discomforting?
5. What negative experiences have you had with change in the past? Have you attempted to make changes or achieve goals, but then failed? How is this contributing to keeping you stuck in your current situation?
6. What stressors do you have the pleasure of avoiding by remaining in your comfort zone?
7. What immediate sources of gratification or rewards do you experience by staying in your current situation?
8. What is it about your comfort zone that you don't want to give up?

Are there any other benefits of remaining in your current situation that you want to add to your list? You should now have a good understanding of how staying in your comfort zone and not taking action is providing you with some kind of pay-off, benefit, or plain old comfort.

You should also know that you are doing what you are doing right now, because you associate it with pleasure. Comfort = pleasure. Even if you know you shouldn't be doing what you're doing or staying in the circumstances or comfort zone that you're in, it has many advantages that *make you feel good.*

As you examine your current situation, your goal is to experience more frustration than pleasure. When you can recognize that the disadvantages of your current situation clearly outweigh the advantages, then you are more likely to increase your commitment to your future goal. Your goal is to reach the point where you no longer think of your current behaviours or lifestyle as desirable and pleasurable. You must find a way to replace the positive experience of your comfort zone. Let me leave you with this perspective: How on earth can you be comfortable, knowing that you're in a state of inaction? You're either growing and moving forward or you're shrinking and becoming stagnant. Which is it going to be?

CHAPTER 8

Committing to the Future: Achieving Your Goal

COMMITMENT TO THE FUTURE: ACHIEVING YOUR GOAL

The second stage of goal-setting achievement involves committing to your future goal. Have you ever had a goal that you started, but didn't seem to be able to commit to achieving? Maybe you had a goal to commit to reading personal development books three evenings per week before bedtime. Maybe you kept at it for a few weeks, and then for some *strange* reason, you gave up or forgot about it. Have you ever felt motivated at one moment with your goal, and then suddenly lost motivation in the next moment? Have you ever saved your money for a few months straight, and then suddenly gone on a spending spree?

This is likely because you have ambivalent thoughts and feelings about achieving your goal. This wavering back and forth occurs because sometimes you are focused on the benefits of saving and at other times all you can focus on is the disappointment of having to refrain from making a purchase. In the Stages of Change Model, the second stage of change is referred to as *contemplation* (Prochaska, Norcross, & Diclemente, 1994) because it involves working out this ambivalence. Likewise, in the second stage of goal-setting achievement, *commitment to the future,* it's important to work through the ambivalence that you have about your goal. Otherwise, you won't be able to stay committed to your goal.

Fortunately, there is a way to solve and work out this ambivalence problem, which involves becoming fully aware of all the positive and negative consequences you'll experience as a result of *committing* to your goals. Raising awareness of one's attitudes and ambivalence towards future goals has been a key factor in promoting successful change and achievement of one's goals (Prochaska, Norcross, & Diclemente, 1994). It will help you eliminate a lot of your ambivalence when the positive consequences associated with your future goal outweigh the negatives.

Committing to Your Goals: Your Future Situation

What's Positive?
(Positive Motivation)

- What are the positive consequences associated with achieving your goal?
- This is the powerful "why" and "purpose" behind your goal that drives you to take action.
- How will your life get better and how will you ultimately benefit?
- You should focus lots of attention here to increase your motivation.

What's Negative?
(Barriers)

- What are the negative consequences associated with achieving your goal?
- What are your limiting beliefs about committing to your goal?
- What are the major barriers that you fear having to face?
- What do you believe you will have to sacrifice or give up?
- Too much unconstructive focus here prevents you from taking action towards your goals.

Finally, once you become aware of the negative mindsets you hold towards your goal, you'll find it easier to commit to your goal, because you'll know ahead of time what to expect and how to overcome your identified barriers. In addition, once you are fully aware of the positive consequences of reaching your goal, you will increase your motivation and create a powerful "why" behind your goal. This means that you will move towards your goal much more quickly, because you'll have powerful and compelling reasons to take action. Once you are fully aware of, and can accept both the positive and negative aspects of both your current and future situation, you'll be in a much better position to commit to your goals and make the necessary changes involved.

Once you complete the following exercises, you should achieve a deeper sense of commitment to your goal, because you will have less ambivalence about moving forward at full speed. You might also feel a greater sense of personal responsibility and ownership, or you might find yourself automatically making better choices that will assist you on your journey.

Ready to get started? Turn the page . . .

NEGATIVE CONSEQUENCES OF YOUR FUTURE SITUATION: COMMITTING TO YOUR GOAL

What *could* be negative if you commit to the achievement of this goal? What happens if you have negative thoughts around the goal that you actually want to move towards? You will push your goal further and further away, because you will feel too much discomfort.

The focus of the next exercise is about identifying all of your negative thoughts, meanings, or consequences associated with the commitment to or achievement of your goal. There are many different ways to understand the different forms of negative thinking. Here are a few to spark your creativity:

- Negative consequences
- Fears
- Barriers
- Poor attitudes
- Worries
- Negative associations
- Bad memories
- Rumours and discouragement from other people regarding what is involved in achieving your goal

Essentially what you are doing is identifying any negative thoughts or "weeds" in your mental garden that will prevent you from committing to or achieving your goal. Remember what I said earlier. We are creatures who will do anything to avoid discomfort in our life, and as a result, we need to remove the discomfort associated with our goals.

This information is valuable to discover, because *any* negative thoughts and beliefs you have towards your goal are going to prevent you from achieving it. For instance, if your goal is to lose weight and get a fit body, you would need to embark on an exercise program. However, what will happen if you associate exercising with *wasting time* or *being sweaty and dirty*? If this plays too large a role in your mind, then you will have a mental barrier or limiting belief that needs to be dealt with. We will work on changing these limiting beliefs in a later section.

Ready to get started? Read through the following questions to identify any negative thoughts you have about working toward your goal.

POWER QUESTIONS

1. Do you fear or avoid having to deal with the potential negative feelings that will come up as you begin committing to your goal? Remember that with the achievement of any goal, less than favourable emotions will be experienced, at least temporarily. Leaving an unhealthy relationship is bound to bring up uncomfortable emotions that one often faces, such as loneliness or fear of not finding another partner. Going back to school or starting a new career or business might also bring up difficult feelings as both you, your family, and your friends adapt to "the new you."

   What do you get to avoid by not taking action towards your goal? Are you avoiding having to deal with frustration, failure, and the anxiety that often comes with it? Consider various writing projects for example. If you've ever written an essay, article, poem, screenplay, or book, then you're probably familiar with reaching the stage when you need to tie many ends together. With all the pressure to meet your deadline and finish off with a piece of work that you will be proud of, you might struggle with feelings of perfectionism or fear of failure. Amongst the fear and pressure, you might worry that you won't produce the quality of work that you want, so you avoid doing any writing at all. To what extent do you experience this type of avoidance with any of your goals?

2. What negative ideas or associations do you have when you think about committing to the achievement of your goal? Do you have any negative memories or past experiences that are associated with achieving your goal?
3. When you think about your goal, are you reminded of any *sacrifices* you'll need to make that you perceive as negative?
4. Do you have any negative associations to any particular *steps* of achieving your goal?
5. What are you not comfortable with when you think about committing to your goal?
6. What is it that you fear about working towards your goal? Do you have a fear that you'll fail or that things won't turn out as perfectly as you'd hoped? Do you fear that you'll invest a lot of money into your dream without receiving the results you'd like? Do you worry about the possibility of it all being a waste of time?
7. Do you spend too much time worrying about what other people will think? Do you worry that you'll look like a fool or not live up to others' expectations?
8. Do you get paralyzed by not knowing where to start? Are you unsure of what information or resources you need? Perhaps you're concerned about those things that you don't know that you don't know. Are you afraid you won't understand things when you begin to educate yourself on something? Do you believe that you need to first be an expert to start something?
9. To what extent are you concerned that you'll start pursuing your dream and goals and then you'll either give up or not follow through?
10. What excuses are you constantly playing through your mind? Do you excuse yourself, because you feel there isn't enough time? Do you let yourself off the hook simply because you don't feel that you have enough knowledge? How do you rationalize giving yourself permission to not work towards and achieve your goals?

Remember, your brain will always attempt to move your behaviours away from negative experiences and towards positive experiences. If the achievement of your goal is even remotely perceived as having any strongly negative aspects involved, then it will be difficult for you to persist with your efforts.

Thus, your goal is to control and minimize your negative ideas, associations, and limiting beliefs that you have about your goal. It's almost impossible to invest yourself in something that you have bad vibes about. This is something we'll be tackling in more depth in the next chapter.

You're either moving away from your goal or towards it, falling down or rising up, or having more negative than positive attitudes towards your goal. Which will it be? In the past, when you've found it difficult to stay committed to your goal, it is because on some level, you have created negative meanings or associations towards the actions that are required for you to achieve the goal. Negative thoughts and ideas about your goal are nothing more than another internal barrier or limiting belief.

Rather than feeling negative when you think about your goal, you need to feel amazingly positive and hopeful. If you are thinking and feeling more negatively about your future achievement as opposed to positive, then you will always experience a lack of motivation, and you will find excuses and reasons to not work towards your goal. Your next task of goal achievement is to examine the benefits you'll experience as a result of achieving your goal. Ready?

WHAT'S SO GREAT ABOUT ACHIEVING THIS GOAL?

Have you ever heard people talk about their big "why" or purpose behind their goal? More often than not, it's a positive force that drives them to achieve their goal. I refer to this as positive motivation. Focusing on the positive consequences of achieving your goal is one of the best sources of motivation you'll ever find!

As a result, your next step is to make a list of all the benefits and positive consequences you will experience if you commit to the achievement of your goal. Your brain is quite intelligent and will only work hard on your goal when there are plenty of good reasons to do so. You want to get yourself to the point where you have so many great advantages and reasons for why you must achieve this goal. So, it's your job to create a compelling list of all the advantages to achieving your goal—all the ways in which you will benefit. The more excited you feel about all these advantages, the more quickly you will move towards your goal.

There are many different ways to think about the positive benefits to achieving your goal. In addition to thinking of benefits, think of the following:

- Achievements
- Positive consequences
- Improvements
- Reasons you want this goal
- Purpose behind the goal
- Rewards
- Recognition
- The "why" behind your goal
- Positive feelings, such as joy, ecstasy, and happiness
- Comfort
- Gains
- Increases

Are you ready to get started creating your own list of how you will benefit if you achieve your goal? Flip the page to review the power questions that will help you stimulate even more positive reasons to achieve your goal.

POWER QUESTIONS

1. How will your life improve once you achieve your goal? Close your eyes for a few moments, and imagine very clearly how your life will be different. What does it look like? Think of as many details as possible. The more vivid the picture you can create, the stronger your desire will become. You might also want to create your own vision board by clipping out pictures that imitate what you are trying to achieve. The more you remind yourself of your goal, the more automatic your actions will become, because the picture is ingrained in your subconscious mind.
2. What is great about achieving your goal? What positive feelings will you have as a result of achieving your goal? Create a list now.
3. How will the achievement of your goal provide you with more momentum and leverage to achieve your other important goals? Have you ever heard of the saying, "When it rains it pours?" The idea is that when an unfortunate event occurs, many other unfortunate events are bound to occur at the same time. Rather than believing this is due to unseen forces of the universe (e.g., the law of attraction), it might also be due to the fact that when a person is feeling under the weather, she is more likely to have a negative attitude and make poor choices in her life. Likewise, when unfortunate events occur that are entirely out of her control, she might perceive those events from a more pessimistic perspective. I believe the same is true for the idea that "all good things come at once." This is because when a person has such a positive attitude and higher self-esteem, as a result of having achieved an important goal,

that person is more likely to step outside of her comfort zone and take more actions towards other important life goals. So, from this perspective, how will achieving one of your major goals positively influence your future goal achievement?

4. How will staying committed to your goal increase your self-esteem? Think carefully about this. If you achieve one of your really important goals, then you will also experience many positive emotions at the same time. Your self-esteem is also likely to increase. As a result, you will have a more positive attitude and outlook on your ability to make life changes and achieve your personal goals in other areas of your life as well.
5. How will your role models—the people you want to work with, become like, or be associated with—view you more favourably once you achieve your goal?
6. How does achieving your goal enable you to give something back to your family, community, or the world at large? Who will you become a role model for once you achieve your goal?
7. How will achieving your goal affect your social network and the people you're able to meet and mingle with each day?
8. What new opportunities or doors will open for you as a result of achieving your goal?
9. What kind of challenge does achieving your goal represent? What will attaining your goal symbolize for you?
10. What excites you about your goal in particular?
11. How will achieving your goal change components of your life in a positive, permanent manner? How will attaining your goal create positive memories for you to look back on? Who will you become as a result of achieving this goal, and how will your character be shaped?

The answers that you think of will be something that you will have forever. Nobody can take away your accomplishments, positive experiences, and memories. Once you have the satisfaction of achieving your goals, you will always strive for something better in your life. You will always want to improve yourself, other people, and the environment around you.

Let's say that through careful analysis you were able to make millions of dollars in the stock market, but then you accidentally lost it all. Although you lost the money, you never lost the knowledge that you accumulated. You will most likely be able to apply the same techniques to your investments again, so that you can create the same results in the future. Likewise, imagine that you built a profitable business that succeeded, but eventually you were beat out by your competitors. You still haven't lost all the knowledge, experience, and important learning lessons that you picked up along the way. No one can take this away from you.

You should now have gained a lot of great insight into the positive and negative associations you have regarding both your current situation and your future goal achievement.

MAXIMIZE THIS . . .

The idea is to maximize your awareness of what is negative about your current situation, so that you can move away from it. You'll also want to focus on the benefits of achieving your goal, so that you attempt to move towards it. Keeping these two focuses in mind will drastically help you to increase your motivation. I refer to this as the "action mindset."

The Action Mindset

The Action Mindset: The Attitude of Motivation	
Positive Motivation What are the amazing benefits to achieving your goal?	**Negative Motivation** What are the negative consequences if you don't achieve your goal?

Positive motivation is about focusing on all the benefits and positivity that you will experience in your life if you stay committed to your goals and if you actually achieve these goals. The more positive reasons you have for achieving your goal, the more motivation you'll have. Negative motivation is about focusing on the pain, risks, and negative consequences you will experience if you don't move away from your current situation. What will happen if you don't commit and take the necessary actions to move towards achieving your goal? Or, if you've already reached your goal, but then lost that achievement, how do you suffer as a result of having to regress to your current state?

MINIMIZE THIS . . .

On the other hand, you are left with the challenge to minimize the positive associations you have of your current situation, as well as the negative associations you have towards achieving your goal. All these associations—the positive ideas about your current comfort zone and the negative ideas regarding your goals—*can be considered limiting beliefs, because they are preventing you from achieving your goals.*

On some level, i.e., unconsciously, you have chosen to make these things mean what they mean. Every thought, attitude, meaning, perspective, and opinion exists because you have constructed it that way. Of course, we cannot always control the circumstances that we find ourselves in, but we can control how we react and deal with these circumstances. This includes being 100 percent responsible for our thoughts, beliefs, and attitudes that we choose to form around everything that is happening in our life.

In order to take responsibility for your belief systems or the meanings that you hold in your mind, you must first become aware of them. We have already done a lot of awareness building around which associations and thoughts are present in our life, for better or worse. Now, we are going to focus on understanding these associations as belief systems. Although there is much overlap between associations and belief systems, when the word "belief" is used, it becomes really obvious that conditioned ways of thinking and associations are also choices. If they are choices, then you can learn to change those associations, meanings, ways of thinking, or beliefs. You have the power to change their meanings. This is what I'm going to show you how to do in the next chapter.

CHAPTER 9

Building the Foundation: Preparation

THE TASK OF PREPARATION: YOUR BELIEFS AND BEHAVIOURS

The third stage of goal-setting achievement is preparation. Similar to the third stage of change from the Stages of Change Model, this involves experimenting with actions, while also getting ready to address barriers (Prochaska, Norcross, & Diclemente, 1994). In the stages of goal setting and achievement, this involves addressing one's limiting belief systems and substituting healthy beliefs. It also involves a fair degree of planning around implementing new behaviours and habits. In order to achieve your goals, it is important for you to lay down the foundation upon which your success will be built.

When most people set goals, they rush into taking action right away. This is most apparent in the New Year. Many people set goals to start investing their money, open a small business, quit smoking, or spend more time with friends and family. They write their goals down with great intentions and suddenly begin executing their actions. There is often no concrete plan involved and little to no preparation. As a result, many people are bound to fail or give up out of frustration.

Did you know that when people are trying to quit a bad habit they set the same New Year's resolution on average ten times before they actually give up that bad habit? (Polivy & Herman, 2002). Why do you think it takes so many attempts? How much preparation and planning do you think went into their goals? A learning lesson is if you don't prepare yourself before launching your goals and the necessary changes behind them, you are likely to fail or to only succeed for a short period of time.

There are two main tasks that need to be addressed in the preparation stage of goal-setting achievement, in order for you to be successful in achieving your goals. This involves identifying the beliefs and behaviours that hold you back, and then being able to change them, so that they support you. Once you have a set of beliefs and behaviours that are stable, automatic, and supportive of your goals, success and achievement will become more natural and easier. However, this takes work. Some people hire a psychotherapist, hypnotist, life coach, or business coach. Others spend hundreds of dollars on self-help books and audio programs, and also attend personal development seminars and conferences.

Whatever approaches you use to help you achieve your goals, there is always something systematic happening behind the scenes of your self-change endeavours. This work includes changing your beliefs and behaviours. I know what you're thinking—the same thing that a lot of people might be thinking at this stage. *This sounds like a lot of work*. Of course it is. If it weren't, then everybody would be happily in the process of achieving their life goals.

It is a myth, however, that achieving goals simply requires a lot of willpower. For instance, when you hear about the person who is taking night classes in the evenings, or the person who spends hours each night developing her business on the side, you might be tempted to think, *that person must have a lot of willpower and self-discipline*. To some extent she does, but even more important is that she has developed certain perspectives, attitudes, life philosophies, or beliefs that eventually make her mindset and actions automatic. In other words, she executes her goals with ease for the most part. This reinstates the importance of taking the time to prepare for your actions.

Keep in mind that the more prepared you are, the more likely you are to make greater progress in achieving your goals, sooner rather than later. Very rarely is there such a thing as instant success. When you read or watch success stories in the media, or watch movies and read books, what is often left out is all the hard work and previous steps of action that were taken throughout the years. Success is something that evolves throughout time. You must be patient.

Even after you have achieved a goal, or made progress towards your goal, you can expect there will be times when you will indulge in actions that seem to sabotage part of your efforts or achievements. This is because changing our actions and moving towards our goals require new ways of thinking and acting that we weren't previously accustomed to. Whenever you feel like you are slacking off or not taking things as seriously as you'd like, you need to return to these key steps involved in achieving your goal. This will involve completing or reviewing these exercises several times, each time to a lesser extent, as your mindset and habits become stronger.

Are you ready to begin identifying your limiting beliefs and learning how to change them, so they support your success? Let's get started on building your foundation for success.

CHAPTER 10

Identifying Beliefs That Hold You Back

IDENTIFYING AND CHANGING LIMITING BELIEFS

> Choose your thoughts no differently than you would choose your friends and soul mate – carefully!

When you begin to identify all your limiting beliefs or ways of thinking that have limited you,—remember that your beliefs are what create your own reality. A limiting belief is simply a thought or belief that prevents you from moving towards your goals.

There are many different pieces of language used when referring to a belief. Here are a few alternative ways of talking about beliefs:

- Thoughts
- Ideas
- Personal meanings
- Associations
- Interpretations
- Life philosophies
- Reasons
- Excuses

Regardless of our way of thinking about our goals and life, our beliefs and mindsets can play tricks on us, and actually fool us into *not* achieving our important goals. How does this work?

THE SCARY SECRET ABOUT YOUR MIND

The scary secret about your mind is that when it comes to achieving new goals, it doesn't always have your best interests in mind. This is hard to believe when you identify with your mind, are intimately attached to your thoughts, and "believe in yourself." As a result, questioning your beliefs and ways of thinking can at first feel as though you are betraying yourself, because you simply cannot imagine thinking about your situation in any other way.

One of my clients, who owned her own business, believed that she didn't have enough time or "people resources" to take a two-week vacation during the summer. This belief was *real* to her, and thus, it created her *reality.* What kept her belief alive and strong were her justifications or reasons behind her belief. She believed that if she wasn't there for a period of two weeks that she would lose her customers to competitors during that time. She thought that she would be perceived as a lazy business owner who didn't care about her customers. She also had the excuse that successful business owners don't take any time off work, ever. She was able to "back-up" her reasons and excuses 100 percent, and fully explain to me why she had no time. She believed in her reasons. Therefore, these reasons created her reality.

The scary secret my client was forced to realize was that just because her belief *was in fact her reality*, it was nevertheless holding her back and preventing her from finding a way to make her vacation a reality. Our most intimate and trusted beliefs can be our worst enemy when it comes to achieving something extraordinary. Even though my client had 100 percent valid justifications, stories, excuses, and logical reasons which all made perfect sense to both her and me, it was important for me to help her realize that there was a bigger picture behind all this.

THE BIG PICTURE TO "GET" ABOUT BELIEFS

The bigger picture to understand is that there is no such thing as a belief that is based upon an accurate reality or not. There is no such thing as an accurate versus inaccurate belief, or a right versus wrong belief. Instead, a belief either serves you or it doesn't. A belief either empowers you or disempowers you. A belief either moves you closer to your goals or further away. Looking at the bigger picture means looking at whether or not your belief is enabling you to move forward with your goals. In the case of my client, she realized that her belief was holding her back from achieving what she really wanted—a vacation. As a result, my aim was to help my client find new ways to view her dilemma.

The learning lesson is to not get caught up in whether your belief is true or not, because that is not the game you need to concern yourself with. Of course, your belief is true to you, because it is a way of coping with life circumstances, based on your previous life experiences and conditioning.

BELIEF SYSTEMS AS COPING MECHANISMS

Sometimes, it's empowering to think of beliefs as self-selected coping skills and tools that help a person adapt to her environment. Whether you barely survive, comfortably adapt, or succeed in reaching your personal dreams, it all depends on how well your beliefs help you cope with what your external environment presents you with. In other words, the degree to which you will succeed with your goals depends on how much your beliefs or mental coping strategies support the achievement of your goal.

If a belief is a way to cope, a way to be in charge of your life, and to achieve your goals, then you only need to consider how well your beliefs are helping you get what you want out of life. Are your current belief systems helping you achieve your life dreams? Do they empower or limit you?

In my previous example, the belief or excuse that my client had no time to take a vacation was limiting her, because it prevented her from getting what she really wanted. She was putting up her own blocks to her goal. Her excuses only *excused her* from achieving her important goal. I don't know about you, but I find it scary that our minds can so easily and automatically *excuse ourselves* from something so important to us. But it can happen if we're not fully aware of this and if we fail to take control of our reality.

Your beliefs are either helping you to take further actions towards your goal, or your beliefs are keeping you stagnant or in slow motion. Your thoughts either help you grow or they limit you. If a belief keeps you trapped in a reality that you aren't happy with, then you need a new way to cope or a new belief system. It's that simple. This is the bigger picture to get.

What a woman thinks, believes, and affirms to herself dictates who she is and what results she achieves in life.

EXAMPLES OF COMMON LIMITING BELIEFS

Here are some examples of common limiting beliefs that tend to creep up in the different areas of our life. See if you can relate to any of them.

Career

1. I can't find a career that would allow me to have six weeks of vacation per year.
2. I'll never be able to make a living by doing what I love.
3. You can't get ahead in your career unless you work hard with long hours.
4. I'm too old and not smart enough to start a new career.
5. I don't have time to get an education.
6. I consulted with an expert and she told me it wasn't feasible.
7. I've already pursued this ambition a few times, and nothing ever worked.
8. I don't have the right training or education.
9. I don't live in the right geographical location for this.
10. I don't know where to begin.

Money and Business

1. I can't afford to go to Hawaii.
2. I will never get ahead financially. I will never achieve financial freedom.

2. I don't have the money to turn my sewing hobby into a part-time business.
3. Money isn't important.
4. If it sounds too good to be true, it probably is.
5. Money doesn't affect a person's happiness.

Personal

1. I don't have control over my life circumstances.
2. Relationships don't last forever.
3. People don't give without a hidden intention.
4. It's better to be a giver than a receiver.
5. I will never be happy and content with my life.
6. I'm too old, too young, not smart enough, not popular enough, not attractive enough, or too timid.

Health

1. It's impossible for me to maintain or lose weight.
2. I can't enjoy my life while being on a diet. Restricting myself is depressing.
3. Exercising every day is unrealistic and obsessive.
4. I cannot find time to exercise, while working a full-time job and raising a family.

You might also find yourself using the following pieces of language as part of your limiting beliefs:

- I can't. I'm not able to.
- I should / I shouldn't
- I have to / I must
- I can only do this *if* . . .
- I need . . .

BELIEFS "COLOUR" OUR WORLD

Another thing to remember about beliefs is that they are our personal constructions of reality. Beliefs are mental creations that protect and defend our present situations. They colour our world by giving our life meaning and helping us make sense of reality by providing us with structured, routine ways to understand our life experiences. Beliefs allow us to experience and recreate in the external world what we have already created in our inner world. Knowing what to expect in the external world gives us safety, comfort, and predictability. Having our assumptions validated in the real world makes us feel intelligent and savvy.

LIMITING BELIEFS ARE A CHOICE

You must realize that it is a *choice* to hold a certain belief that helps you make sense of your life circumstances. A limiting belief is nothing more than a *chosen* way of coping or thinking about life circumstances, and it acts as a barrier to you achieving your personal goals. If you have a limiting belief standing between you and your goal, your aim should be to replace it with a more empowering belief.

Our brains are similar to computers. We have many limiting beliefs, files, and "viruses" in our minds that prevent us from reaping the rewards of our efforts. The following exercise will help you identify which of your beliefs are actually "viruses" that are preventing you from achieving your goal. You want to "delete" these files that hold you back and relay negative messages to you about achieving your goals.

HOW TO GET RID OF YOUR LIMITING BELIEFS

As we've discussed, there are many different ways to talk about and understand the meaning of a limiting belief. Keeping this in mind, I've included a list of questions below that contain buzz words or cues to help you recall hidden or disguised thinking patterns that are destructive.

Read through the list of questions below to identify your limiting beliefs that prevent you from achieving your goal or that make it too difficult to stay committed to your goal. Carefully check for examples of their presence within your own thinking patterns. Here is an example for how you can label and write down your limiting beliefs:

EXAMPLE

1. (Justification)—I don't have enough time to write a book.
2. (Worry)—I'm afraid that I might lose all my money if I start investing.

   Ready to get started?

POWER QUESTIONS

1. What **excuses or justifications** do you unconsciously or consciously use to **excuse** yourself from having to be accountable and committed to your goal? How do you **justify** staying within your current comfort zone in which you take no action and make no commitments towards your goal? For what **reasons** do you explain your current state of inaction? What justifications might you use to tell yourself that your current situation *isn't so bad after all?*

   Remember, you need to catch how you excuse yourself in order to change your thought pattern. For instance, let's say a person's goal is to purchase a second house as an income property. However, she keeps using the excuse that she doesn't have enough time or money to do so. This may be her reality, but she is using this reason as a way to *excuse* herself from taking action. When it comes to your goals, do you want to excuse yourself or give yourself permission to put your goals on hold? Absolutely not!

What is the "all too well-known" **story** that you tell yourself and others about why you can't do something? What are some other "trance-like" **recurring stories, narratives,** or **mental scripts** that end up blocking your progress? Why have you chosen to strengthen those stories and allow them to excuse you from your desired success?

What logical **excuses** do you hold about your state of "inaction,"—excuses that you firmly believe are barriers that you cannot move past? Even though you think this is your "reality," do you recognize the value and importance of how this "reality" holds you back and limits you? Do you recognize that you are choosing to *excuse* yourself from your own personal success? Do you realize that you are choosing to give these barriers a strong and forceful authority over your success? Remember, an excuse is not a good reason. It is only giving yourself permission to not live up to your potential and to not be successful.

2. What **rules** have you created in your life that could be limiting your ability to start taking action towards your goal(s)? We need to be particularly careful about the rules we create. Some people have created a rule that it is better to give than to receive. How does this affect their life and their ability to achieve their goals? This could create difficulty, because all achievements require other peoples' help. Some people have created rules around what they are allowed to spend their money on. Taking a personal development seminar or course that costs hundreds of dollars is ridiculous to some people in the sense that they've created a rule and put a limit on what they would spend on their continuing education. Check to see

that your rules make sense and will actually help you achieve your goals.

3. What **pessimistic thoughts** recur in your head every time you think about pursuing your dream? Notice which thoughts you allow to hold you back from taking action. Are you blowing something way out of proportion?
4. How do your **expectations** about the process of working on this goal interfere with your motivation or ability to get things moving or done? Perhaps you are hoping to begin a new project, but you have the expectation that you must have large blocks of time to get started. Expectations that are too high can create a sense of paralysis. We all have pictures in our mind of what we think the process of achieving a certain goal should "look" like. How do you know if you have unrealistic expectations? It's simple. Your expectations are too high when they are not assisting you to make progress towards your goals.

   Another language usage similar to expectations is hearing people's **standards** about "what" and "how" things *should* happen. This can sometimes negatively affect their ability to go with the flow, to embrace and accept their current circumstances for what they are. People often wish they could go back to school to obtain more education, or they want to start some kind of business part-time. They feel they don't have the time to do it "just right." Again, this is a standard or expectation that prevents them from taking any action at all towards their goals.

   Are there certain standards or **ideals** that you unconsciously believe you must live by? How might these interfere with you getting the job done?

5. What unnecessary **assumptions** do you make about committing to and achieving this goal? Do you assume that you need someone else's validation or agreement on what you should

or shouldn't do? Do you think that you need **someone else's approval** in order to pursue your goal? Are you looking for your spouse's approval? Are you waiting for your peers or boss at work to cheer you on? Do you look towards the "experts" in your life to give you permission? Do you expect to have excitement and support from those you admire, look up to, or are closest to? Be careful, because *anybody* can discourage you from doing what is most important to you. Don't wait for anybody to give you permission and acceptance to pursue your dreams. Give yourself permission and acceptance to follow your own dreams. Start being your own cheerleader today!

6. What **clichés, quotes, maxims, or catchy phrases** do you entertain in your head that are limiting you? For instance, if you believe you are poor, and you're constantly saying, "The rich only get richer, while the poor get poorer," then you are reinforcing the strength of this limiting belief. If you've identified a limiting belief that making money is hard work, what are the other sayings that go along with or represent this belief? What are the negative sayings that you are holding onto and need to let go of? Here are a few examples: "The rich get richer and the poor get poorer" or "When you have a family, you don't have any time for yourself."

   What **metaphors** do you chant in your head that keep you limited? Consider the metaphor, "Money doesn't grow on trees." If you have this idea alive in your head, and if you think like this on any level, then you are teaching yourself that money cannot come into your life easily.

7. Are there any **values** that you are holding onto that interfere with you achieving this goal? Do you value something that contradicts what you want to move towards? Here is a very common, classic example of what I mean. A common value in our society is to be financially prudent. Unfortunately, there are many goals that do require, sooner or later, a substantial investment of capital. The value of needing to save and spend

very little money can often interfere with a person taking her next action step. To start or expand a business can require a sizeable investment. To produce a professional, functional, and high traffic website can require a good size investment if it is not your specialty. To purchase, renovate, and then flip a property to make a profit requires an investment. Here's a great question to ask yourself when this value of prudence is interfering with your goal. *If I look back at the end of my life, will I regret having made the investment in this goal?*

8. What self-defeating beliefs and meanings have you created, based on your **past failures** with important goals? How do these beliefs limit you from taking risks now?
9. What **evidence** do you focus on to support your own limiting beliefs? Do you gather evidence of others' failures, opinions, and life situations? What **negative memories** of your own do you have that interfere with your confidence and attitude towards achieving your goal? Perhaps you tried pursuing one aspect of your goal in the past, but you "failed." In other words, you reached some kind of barrier or block, and you became overwhelmed and confused.

How is the past preventing you from moving forward in the future? I know in my own life, when I've pursued fairly new and somewhat larger projects, I've easily been discouraged when I've run into roadblocks that I wasn't sure how to overcome. In a lot of cases, my overwhelming feelings led me to push my goal aside. I considered it to be a temporary phenomenon, as I was deciding what to do about the problem. However, I often never came back to resolving the problem, or I delayed for many months, or even years. When I look back on these goals, I have negative memories of not being able to achieve those goals, of feeling too scared, cautious, or even being unfocused or too indecisive. As a result, it can make me quite apprehensive to pursue the same goals again in the future, because I fear making the same mistakes.

It's easy to get focused on the negative aspects and emotions around what happened or didn't happen in the past. I've found that when I experience these negative memories, it really helps me to recall the exact action step that slowed me down. Most often, it was related to not wanting a goal badly enough. Sometimes, it was a result of not having made up my mind on a decision that felt risky or uncomfortable. Sometimes, I was just lacking information to help me make an informed decision, and I never sought out that information. When I recall the exact reasons for not moving forward with these goals, it helps me to minimize the impact of my negative memories and to more easily be able to put them into their proper perspective. So, go ahead and take note of which negative memories might be holding you back.

10. Are there any **disempowering questions** that you continually ask yourself? An example might be the question, "Why does this always happen to me?," which promotes the negative belief that something is actually out of your control. Or, "Why haven't I achieved any of my major life goals by now?"
11. Do you have any **black and white philosophies** also known as "all or nothing" thinking that keep you frozen in a passive way? How does **perfectionist thinking** prevent you from pursuing or staying committed to your goal? What **thoughts** keep you paralyzed, stuck, and lethargic?
12. Where do you fit within the **social norm** *now*, and where *would* you fit if you achieved your goal? How do these thoughts keep you paralyzed or prevent you from committing to your goal? Are you **afraid of achieving more than your loved ones** and those whom you are closest to? What part are you uncomfortable with?
13. What childhood or family **beliefs** have you grown up with that are still a part of your mindset today? What were your parents' attitudes towards pursing their dreams? What messages did you pick up on?

14. What other **myths** do you buy into that prevent you from moving closer towards your goal? Have you been told that you are too young, too old, or that you lack the expertise, a network of people, or time and money needed to achieve your goals?
15. What are the **negative associations** in general that you have about working towards or achieving your goal?
16. How do you limit yourself by believing that you **don't have enough knowledge**, are **not skilled enough**, or simply **do not have enough experience** to reach your goal?
17. What limiting **comparisons** or **analogies** do you frequently catch yourself saying in your head or out aloud?
18. What are your **fears** and/or **worries** that stand between you and your goal?
19. What **self-criticisms** are in place that ensure you don't act on your dreams? What is the negative **self-talk** that comes up every time you get excited about your goal?
20. Do you have any hidden beliefs that what you're doing is somehow **immoral, inappropriate**, or **bad**? What are these beliefs based on and where do they come from?
21. To what extent do you buy into the concept that your efforts might turn into a waste of time? **Are you afraid of the risk** that is involved in pursuing your goal? Do you fear that no matter what you do, you are bound to return to your self-defeating patterns and sabotage your success?

Did you read through all the questions? Below is a listed summary of the different types of limiting thinking, all expressed as different keywords. Scan through this list of words and determine if you have any more limiting beliefs.

How do the following ways of thinking manifest themselves in your thinking patterns? How do these ways of thinking prevent you from achieving your goal?

MORE LIMITING WAYS OF THINKING

Review the following potential limiting ways of thinking and determine which ones you identify with, and how. Write these limiting beliefs down in your journal.

- beliefs
- justifications
- excuses
- reasons
- thoughts
- stories
- rules
- pessimistic thoughts
- ideals
- mental script
- analogies
- social norms
- values
- evidence
- expectations
- schemas
- quotes
- narratives
- mental thought cycles/patterns
- mental pictures
- philosophies
- questions
- assumptions
- standards
- perfectionist thoughts
- comparisons
- visualizations
- metaphors
- aphorisms / maxims
- clichés

- myths
- catchy phrases
- negative associations
- negative memories
- personal intentions
- mental scenery
- similes, idioms, or puns
- worries
- limiting or lack of knowledge
- perspective
- messages received
- family beliefs
- morals
- images
- media messages
- fears
- self-criticisms
- mental "blueprint"
- conditioned thoughts
- motivations
- attempting to prove . . .
- past failures
- self-talk
- affirmations
- any other ways of thinking or cognitions

IS YOUR BELIEF GROUNDED IN REALITY?

Now that you have identified beliefs or ways of thinking that do not serve you well, it's time to find contradictory evidence of these beliefs, so that they no longer have a negative effect over you. In other words, you want to challenge and question your limiting beliefs and identify all the pieces of evidence that run counter to these beliefs. The more awareness that you have around how your thinking patterns are limiting you, the easier it will be to change them.

As you read through the following questions, identify one of your limiting beliefs, and make a list of evidence that contradicts your belief.

POWER QUESTIONS

1. What **evidence** do you have that doesn't support your limiting belief? What are the **exceptions** to your limiting belief? Was there ever an instance in which your belief or way of thinking wasn't helpful, true, or didn't apply to your situation? (This question is a classic one in cognitive-behavioural therapy, which is scientifically proven to be an effective way of ridding oneself of limiting thoughts.)
2. **What is the origin** of your belief? Where did it come from? Was it even your own belief, or did you adopt a cultural message or another person's belief? How did you pick up this way of thinking? Did this way of thinking help or hinder the other people who held it?
3. Is your belief serving a **worthwhile purpose**? Or is it more destructive than useful? Perhaps it served a particular purpose at one time in your life, but now it is unneeded. You could even try making a list of the pros and cons of continuing to hold onto your belief. Write down all the ways in which your belief or thought pattern is helping you. What does the belief do for you? Then, write down all the ways that your belief limits you.
4. How is your way of thinking **ridiculous or absurd**? What is completely irrational about your belief?
5. If you continue to hold onto your belief or way of thinking, what will the **long-term consequences** be? *Hint:* Do any of the people close to you have this belief? What results or experiences did they have in their life as a result of holding onto this belief long-term?

6. How is your belief or thought only a **product of society's status quo?** Try thinking of your belief as a virus, or a cold—something that you "caught." Now, it's your job to fight the virus and return to your previous state of mental health. Do you remember what your mindset was like before you adopted this belief?

IDENTIFYING NEW EMPOWERING BELIEFS

Is it really possible to replace our old beliefs with new ones? Absolutely! A new way of thinking is one that *works* for you on an experiential level. In other words, you do not have to convince yourself of the new way of believing. It should simply make sense to you, or perhaps even feel like you have gained a new insight.

Finding new ways of thinking is a creative process. There is no right or wrong—only a way of thinking that works for you.

There is no *easy* way or "one size fits all" recipe to create an empowering belief or way of thinking that can replace your old ones. This is a creative brainstorming process that requires searching for new meanings that make sense to *you*, and only you. This is a highly personal exercise. Ways of thinking that work for one person might not work for another. For instance, let's say you've identified your limiting belief that you're too old to go back to school. Your friends and family might cheer you on, telling you that age is irrelevant and that pursuing a higher education is even more rewarding when one is older, because one is wiser and can appreciate the value of the experience even more. However, this meaning or perspective might not do anything for you. Instead, a person would be better off coming up with her own personalized meaning, such as, "Whether or not I pursue this education, time is going to pass me by. I might as well have the time pass me by and accomplish a lot at the same time." This way of thinking might override the person's old belief or excuse of being too old.

For the second part of this exercise, you are challenged to discover new, empowering ways of thinking—ones that can **replace** your old ways of thinking. Do not simply write down how you *think* you *should* think. This is NOT good enough. Your new way of thinking must make sense and be real and believable for you. If your new way of thinking is only a *should,* then you have not truly found a new way of thinking that will stick.

I highly recommend that, not only do you complete this exercise by writing your new beliefs down on paper, but even more important, that you keep this information in a safe place. You will want to review this information on a regular basis to remind yourself of your new ways of thinking that will help you achieve your goal.

> *Choosing a new belief system is a bit like choosing a piece of artwork. It's completely personal and it's all about finding a way of thinking that inspires you.*

Here is another example:

Old Way of Thinking:

(Justification)—I'm too self-conscious to take a public speaking course.

New Way of Thinking:

(Self-talk)—The point of taking the public speaking course is to practice my speaking, so that I can become less self-conscious. By focusing on my self-consciousness, I'm only making my situation worse.

POWER QUESTIONS

Read through the following questions to help you think of new belief systems. When your new way of thinking really resonates with you, jot it down.

1. How can you justify your new belief? What strong reasons do you have that support your new way of thinking?
2. What attitude or outlook will you need to have in order to be able to take risks, while feeling security at the *same* time? For a few years, one of my goals was to finally publish my first book. One thing that was holding me back was making an investment in hiring a team of people who could assist me with the process. In my mind, it seemed like such a big risk to spend a chunk of money on something that, at the end of the day, would have no guarantee of a return on my investment. We all have bigger purchases that we want to make, but often we might feel a pressure that we should be conservative. Or we feel that we are being too self-indulgent. Eventually, I found a new outlook or perspective. That was my turning point. I realized that this investment was much different than the many other purchases that were on my "wish list." This one was very much in line with my values. I imagined myself looking back on my decision, after my goal was achieved. I reflected on whether or not I would feel regret about the decision. I even imagined myself at the end of my life, looking back on this goal and assessing whether or not it was worth it. These ways of thinking made me realize how important and personal this goal was for me to achieve. Finally, after much going "back and forth," I decided to make the commitment. The point is that sometimes, you just need to realize how your goal is in line with your true values. Once you align them, you will experience much more motivation to move forward with your goals and with a lot of action.
3. What analogies can you think of that would counteract your old belief and support your new belief?

4. What new rules or standards do you want to hold yourself to regarding your goal?
5. Can you experience any comfort in your process of change and achievement by acknowledging which actions or steps are only temporary? Which actions/efforts will not last forever with regards to your efforts?

   Perhaps you are debating whether or not you should go back to college or university, but you are concerned about the large commitment of time involved. You might try taking comfort in the perspective that your investment is only a one-time investment. You could also decide to spread your course work out, so that you could go part-time.

   Are you trying to quit one of your bad habits? Take consolation in knowing that the difficulty involved in the beginning is only temporary. Anything that you achieve for the first time, and any habit that you attempt to create for the first time is always the most difficult.

6. What assumptions could you make that would make the attainment of your goal a lot easier?
7. What way of thinking will motivate you the most?
8. What self-talk would the stronger part of you that is nurturing, parental, and supportive, want to offer?
9. How would a person who has already achieved this goal think?
10. What affirmations could you find or create that would be conducive to achieving your goal?

Ready to develop your own new ways of thinking that will replace your limiting beliefs? Just remember, as you practice this exercise, you will get much better at it. Write your new set of beliefs in your journal.

New belief systems must click and fit with the authentic you. Only then, will they make a true impression upon your subconscious mind.

STRENGTHENING YOUR NEW BELIEFS

You have now identified a bunch of new, empowering belief systems. Hopefully, they really "click" with you on a cellular level and make complete sense. This still doesn't promise or ensure 100 percent that you will always behave and think in ways based on your belief. It's important to identify and gather many good reasons that support your new belief as being "correct" or worthy of believing in.

Belief systems are rarely a matter of what is right or wrong. Rather, it's about what works and produces the results that you are looking to experience in your life.

Once you have found beliefs that you are confident will produce great results, you need to build and strengthen these belief systems.

It might first be helpful to describe what a belief system is. Anthony Robbins describes a belief as something for which you have evidence. He uses a great analogy of a table with four legs (Robbins, 1991). The table top could be considered the belief, while the legs are the evidence that supports the table top or the belief. The stronger the legs are, and the more legs that you have supporting your belief, the stronger your belief will be. The more this belief makes sense to you, the more you will live it out in your life. Thus, you want to find as much evidence as possible for your beliefs or ways of thinking that empower you.

POWER QUESTIONS

Here are some questions to help you strengthen your belief systems. Choose one empowering belief to start with, and ask yourself these questions. Eventually, you will want to do the same with each of your new beliefs.

1. What evidence do you have to support this new way of thinking?
2. What sorts of behaviours, activities, or actions could you take that would strengthen this belief?
3. What symbols or rituals would build your belief and make it stronger?
4. What self-talk would be conducive to strengthening this belief system?
5. How would you need to talk to other people about yourself to strengthen this belief?
6. What language or sayings could you use that would make this belief stronger?

For instance, in Michael Losier's wonderful book *The Law of Attraction,* (Losier, 2003) he discusses the power that language has in attracting desires. Michael encourages people to use the phrase, "I am in the process of . . ." This has been extremely useful for me in my life. For instance, you might say, "I am in the process of building a positive attitude about my life." This is believable for a lot of people, because even though they haven't arrived at their goals yet, they are at least on the journey or path to solidifying their habits of positive thinking. I highly recommend Michael's book (go to www.LawofAttractionBook.com) to give you more ideas on the power of language and how selecting the appropriate words or language can affect your level of success.

EXAMPLE

Old Way of Thinking:

(Justification)—I'm too self-conscious to take a public speaking course.

New Way of Thinking:

(Self-talk)—The point of taking the public speaking course is to practice my speaking, so that I can become less self-conscious. By focusing on my self-consciousness, I'm only making my situation worse.

Reasons That Support the New Belief:

- If I can just learn even one or two tips in the public speaking course, I will reduce my self-consciousness and taking the personal risks will have been worth it.
- Even if I don't improve my public speaking that much, I will feel better knowing that I've done everything I can to improve upon my public speaking. I will be less likely to feel like a victim.

Now, it's your turn to write down reasons and pieces of evidence that support your new way of thinking. Pull out your journal.

CHAPTER 11

What Are Your Bad Habits?

WHICH OF YOUR HABITS SLOW DOWN YOUR GOAL ACHIEVEMENT?

> A change in bad habits leads to a change in life.
> -Jenny Craig

I once heard that success is the result of the accumulation of many excellent habits. For years, I took this advice for granted, but now I realize that having excellent habits really is the cornerstone of success. I also adopt the perspective that we are only as strong as our weakest link when it comes to our habits. Having one really bad habit in place is enough to hold a person back from achieving an important goal. For this reason, we must identify which bad habits are holding us back.

Remember, just as we have thought patterns that don't serve us well, we also have behavioural patterns that we might not even be aware of in terms of how they prevent us from reaching our goals. There are many ways to think about habits and behaviours, and many words to describe them. Here are some examples:

- Actions
- Sabotaging behaviours
- Avoidant actions
- Things that you *do not* do
- Ways of living
- Activities
- Habits
- Patterns or cycles
- Procrastinating
- Rebellious behaviours

The purpose of the following questions is to help you identify any habits or behaviours that will prevent you from achieving your goal, or that will slow down the process. We must first become aware of what these limiting behaviours are, so that we can unlearn them and then create new habits.

POWER QUESTIONS

1. What self-defeating behaviours do you engage in? Do you only get five hours of sleep per night during the week, and then spend your weekend days sleeping in until the afternoon? Also, examine how your self-defeating behaviours negatively affect some of your other behaviours or lack of behaviours.
2. Do you have any patterns around how you sabotage any of your efforts? For instance, perhaps you stick to a savings plan for two months, and then you find yourself spending like crazy in the third month. The end result is as though you had been overspending all along.
3. Which of your behaviours has the strongest negative impact on your goal? In other words, if you could make just one single and powerful change to your habits, what would it be?
4. Can you identify any behavioural cycles or patterns that hold you back? What behaviour is the trigger or catalyst to this pattern? For instance, once I was working with a client who shared that she tended to switch companies every five years. When I asked her why, she stated that as soon as people expected more of her, she was uncomfortable at living up to their expectations and not able to address the conflict that inevitably arose. In my client's mind, it was easier to simply start the pattern all over again at a new company. Unfortunately, this pattern prevented her from advancing into senior management positions and from gaining a certain amount of expertise in one area. The trigger that scared her was conflict and fear of failure of not meeting others' expectations.
5. Which behaviours end up making you feel the worst? For instance, which behaviours make you feel the most sad, angry, guilty, or lethargic after engaging in them?
6. Which behaviours are holding you back from achieving your goals?
7. What activities or pursuits do you engage in as a useless or detrimental distraction? For instance, do you go shopping and

spend too much money just because you are bored? Do you date all the wrong people just to keep yourself busy and comfortable?

8. What **do you *not* do** that holds you back? What sorts of things **do you avoid on a regular basis** that make your progress more difficult? How does lack of planning prevent you from moving closer to your goals? Do you have a bad habit of not asking for help in the areas where you probably need it the most? Does your avoidance of communication with your partner or boss prevent you from moving forward? Do you avoid scheduling important tasks in your calendar?

Keeping your answers to these questions in mind, use your journal to write down any of your limiting behaviours or habits, because the next step involves figuring out how to replace them with new habits.

MILLION DOLLAR HABITS!

Imagine if you could identify the habits that would be the keys to your success. All success boils down to having great habits. When was the last time you identified what these successful habits would be for you?

People are always good at identifying what behaviours, actions, or habits are *bad*. But how many people ever sit down with a notebook to reflect on powerful behaviours or actions that they could substitute for their previous behaviours? Doing this can give you a *lot* of leverage and momentum. It's much easier to get rid of a habit when you have a new habit to substitute for it.

Habits are the building blocks on which we achieve our milestones, goals, life dreams, and success in general.

THE POWER OF ROUTINES

An important lesson on the theory of goal setting that you'll want to take away from sports psychology involves the implementation of routines in your life. Who would have thought that such a basic principle could be so powerful?

Women with powerful routines have learned how to automate their achievement and success.

Here's a quick exercise for you to try. Think about anything in your life right now that gives you a consistent source of pleasure. How does this become so? There is probably some routine of behaviours behind it.

For instance, if your career gives you pleasure, it's because you have a routine or habit in place of going to work several times a week. If your relationships with others consistently give you pleasure, then you probably have a habit of making plans and seeing them regularly. If your health and fitness levels give you joy, it's obvious that you have a routine behind that as well. Routines are nothing more than an accumulation of habits or behaviours that you have made automatic.

Here is a very powerful quote that I want to expand on: **"Routines are one of the most effective ways to systematically plan for success. Routines have been shown to be invaluable in helping athletes achieve their competitive goals" (Schack, Whitmarsh, Pike, Redden,** 2005, p. 138).

So, what does this mean to you? Many sports psychology theories that apply to athletic performance can also apply to our everyday performance in life. Just as Olympians want to break new world records, we as individuals want to reach new performance records within the different areas of our own life. All of our goals involve us "performing," or behaving and thinking in certain disciplined ways to reach our goals.

If you want to change the results in your life, change your habits and routines.

BREAKING YOUR GOALS DOWN INTO ROUTINES

We often hear that we should break all our goals down into a series of actions. Well, on a parallel note, another great theory of goal setting is to **break your goals down into a series of mini routines.**

In other words, what routines do you need to get into the habit of following on a consistent basis if you are to achieve your goals?

For example, if we take a common pursuit of wanting to eat healthily, this is easy to think of in terms of routines:

- Scheduling in and reminding oneself of when one will buy groceries
- Planning one's meals and snacks ahead of time
- Writing a detailed grocery list ahead of time of which groceries are needed
- Consistently grocery shopping at the same time each week, e.g., each Monday morning
- Washing and chopping up vegetables as soon as groceries are bought
- Spending fifteen minutes each evening to make a salad for the next day at work
- And so on . . .

See how the seemingly simple goal of eating healthy foods requires a lot of planning and action steps? If you can use this theory of goal setting and make these steps part of **an automatic routine,** then you will have a lot going in your favour.

LEARNING LESSONS FROM SPORTS PSYCHOLOGY

In sports, routines have helped athletes to cope better and to reduce external stressors and distractions when they are in an important competition. We can borrow a few lessons from sports psychology, because every day we are faced with external distractions, barriers, or environmental influences that can distract us from focusing on our goals. There are a few key **benefits to having routines in our life.**

First, when you are focused on routines that support your goals, you are less likely to be distracted by pursuing other activities that you don't value. Often, a barrier to achieving one's goals is getting distracted by other activities. Once a routine is established, it is a powerful, automatic way of staying focused on your goals.

So, what routines do you have in place? Do they lead you and guide you? Do they keep you focused on what is most important? Do they lead you through uncertain or stressful times? Do you have a habit of "falling off the wagon" with your goals when you face barriers? You can see how important the power of routines truly is.

Secondly, routines can give you a sense of familiarity and comfort as you pursue your goals in life. Routines are a series of behaviours that are in your control. When athletes arrive at a new location for a competition, the one thing in their control is that they have a series of mental and physical warm-up routines to follow. No matter what other external barriers arise in their external environment, they do have something in their own control—their routine. This routine keeps them focused.

Apply this same principle to your own life. No matter what comes up in your life, such as stressors, unexpected circumstances, or any other challenges, you can control the fact that you can implement routines that, not only allow you to survive, but also help you thrive.

You might have heard the following saying: *It is not what happens to us, but it is how we respond to what happens to us.* There will always be unexpected "roadblocks" that come up during the pursuit of our goals. However, if we have a solid, strong routine that feels good to us, we'll have that as our foundation to fall back on.

Routines are the building blocks with which we can create an ecstatic life and strive for our lofty goals. As the saying goes, you cannot build a house on a rocky foundation. The same is true with your life goals. You cannot achieve greatness without a solid foundation of strong routines that support you throughout all of life's challenges.

PERSISTING WITH YOUR NEW HABITS

The best way to think about making your habits and actions automatic is to remember when you first learnt to drive a vehicle. At first, it required a lot of conscious effort, but now you don't even need to think about it. You just drive easily and automatically. Or think of another behaviour you tried to change (e.g., quitting smoking, cutting sugar or caffeine out of your diet) that was very difficult in the beginning, but then later became easier until it was automatic. The same is true with being in the driver's seat of your own life, and being in control of your destiny. At first, any goal requires a lot of concentration and hard work. There will be times when you don't believe you'll make it. But you have to keep persisting, and eventually, your new habits will stick.

> *Habits work because they automatically focus our energy, creating a harmonious flow or channelling of our energy, which leads to the results we desire.*

READY TO REFLECT ON YOUR NEW HABITS?

The next exercise is intended to help you identify new and alternative behaviours to replace the limiting behaviours that you just identified in the last exercise. Don't forget to think of unique and significantly robust behaviours that you could *add* to your lifestyle regardless of what behaviours you get rid of. Be radical and have fun with this exercise. Your next step is to answer the following list of questions to ensure that you've exhausted all of your ideas on how you can have successful habits. Good luck!

POWER QUESTIONS

1. What new empowering behaviours or habits can you add to your lifestyle that would replace your limiting behaviours?
2. When you observe people who have already achieved a goal similar to yours, what behaviours do they seem to incorporate into their life?
3. How can you be "lazy" and relax a lot, while still moving forward with your goal? How can you do less, while creating more abundance and joy? Be creative here. Often, people believe that reaching their goals requires working longer and harder. This doesn't need to be the case. Whatever your goal is, there will be steps or times when you will need the assistance of other people or services. For example, let's say that your goal is to open a part-time business, selling fresh baked goods. After you exhaust a list of all the activities involved, you might feel a bit overwhelmed. It is often helpful to think about which tasks could be delegated to others or outsourced. What strategies could you implement, so that you could work less and achieve more?
4. How can you take action and have fun and be productive at the same time? How can you make your efforts and action steps more convenient to carry out? These questions are really tapping into the idea of planning ahead. When would be the best time of day, or the best time of the week to carry out your action steps? For instance, let's say you have a goal to exercise daily. When is the best time for you to exercise? Would you feel the most comfortable planning to get your exercise in before the start of your workday? Or would you

be the most motivated and energetic after work? Also, which time is most convenient for you? Which habit are you most likely to stick with?

Let's say your goal is to make sure that you buy healthy groceries every week, despite the fact that you dread grocery shopping. Ask yourself, "How can I make this fun?" Perhaps you might choose a grocery store that has a pleasant environment. Maybe you'll decide to purchase a hot tea and enjoy sipping on your tea, as you pick out your groceries. Be outrageous. Whatever can improve the experience of your habits, and even make it a bit fun, will drastically help you stick to your goals.

If your goal is to keep your house tidy and wash your dishes daily, again, how could you turn this into a pleasurable experience? Here's how I personally have kept this somewhat enjoyable. I bought a pair of gloves, since I cannot stand the thought of my hands becoming dried out from dish soap. The thought of putting my nicely manicured hands into dirty dishwater was definitely not in my comfort zone. No wonder I avoided doing this chore so often. Sometimes, changing the small things can make a really big difference in our motivation to take action. In my case, once I had new gloves, I decided to wash my dishes when I came home from work, as it was a great way for me to clear my head and do something a bit "meditative."

5. What can you do that will enrich your experience of carrying out the necessary habits or action steps that you dread?
6. How can you make stepping outside of your comfort zone convenient and comfortable? Does your goal involve having to talk to and meet new people? Will networking be a considerable part of your goal? I've worked with several clients in the past, who decided to increase their interpersonal confidence by improving their personal image. Whenever they

would need to go to a conference or networking meeting, they were able to feel better about the situation by focusing on creating a superb image. They bought new professional attire that made them feel like "a million bucks." All of the little appearance items that they had previously taken for granted, they now paid attention to. This way, they knew they were putting their best foot forward, and doing everything in their control to increase their comfort around meeting and talking to new people. As a result, they found a way to make their new habit of networking something they enjoyed and actually looked forward to.

7. What action would give you the most leverage to achieve your goal?
8. What behaviours could you take advantage of *now* that would give you momentum?
9. What sorts of actions could you include on this journey that would make achieving your goal fun or easy? How can you incorporate the needed tasks or steps for achieving this goal in a *convenient* manner?
10. How could you achieve this goal in the quickest way possible, *while also* producing the highest quality results?
11. What behaviours, actions, or habits have you typically never tried when it comes to achieving this sort of goal?

YOU CAN DO THIS!

You should now have identified all of the new behaviours that you want to engage in. Congratulations! The next step is to find "evidence" or reasons that you can carry these actions out. For instance, let's say your goal is to be up at 6 a.m. each morning to read a personal development book. You know you want to do this, but you doubt your ability to be disciplined or motivated. You know that when your alarm clock goes off, the chances of you turning it off and going back to sleep are great. From another perspective, you might worry that you will use "getting to bed late" as an excuse. Either way, you have doubt.

DUMP YOUR DOUBT

Think of your doubts as toxic waste products. Having waste in your body is toxic, and it will slow you down incredibly. The same is true with your goals. You must get rid of as much doubt and uncertainty as possible, so that you can move forward with very high confidence. Although it is natural to always have some degree of doubt, we can do our best to keep it to a minimum.

Here's an example from one of my clients and how she diminished her doubt that she couldn't get up at 6:00 a.m. to read her personal development books. Take careful note of her positive mindsets.

EXAMPLE:

- I am always able to get up at 6 a.m. when I have early morning meetings. Thus, getting up at the same time to do something that I find really exciting should be a "piece of cake."

- A few of my colleagues are up this early simply to read the newspaper, so if they can do that, surely I can motivate myself to get up and read something that will actually increase my productivity throughout the day.

- Although once in a while, I will be short on sleep as a result of getting up so early, I recognize that I cut my sleep short for other things that are less important than my personal development, i.e., surfing the internet late at night.

In Michael Losier's (2003) book *The Law of Attraction*, he states that, "allowing is the absence of doubt" (p. 72). He gives examples of "allowing statements," that I interpret to be similar to finding evidence that you can achieve your goals. An allowing statement for my example might be something like, "Thousands of successful women around the world are already getting up at 6 a.m. each morning to read personal development books," and "Thousands of people each day are creating a new habit of getting up that early to invest in their personal growth." The point is if other people can do it, so can you!

BE RADICAL WITH YOUR EVIDENCE

Go nuts and gather whatever evidence it takes, so you can achieve this goal. Remember, you don't have to read this list to other people. Be creative, and let your ideas flow. Create your list of evidence now. Have fun!

CHAPTER 12

Momentum and Engagement

REVIEW OVER AND OVER AGAIN

Now you've completed the tasks involved in the preparation stage of goal-setting achievement. You've identified and changed your beliefs and behaviours that aren't conducive to your success, and you should now have improved substitutions in your thinking and habits. I highly recommend that you continue to review your list of new beliefs. You might even refer to your new beliefs as affirmations, which are positive statements that will reinforce and strengthen your efforts to continue taking action with your goals. Likewise, continue to review your list of new habits to remind yourself of these actions. Post both of these lists somewhere you will see them every day.

KEEPING UP THE MOMENTUM

The fourth stage of goal-setting achievement is *momentum*. Momentum is all about continuing to take action with your goals. In the original Stages of Change Model, this was referred to as the *action stage* (Prochaska, Norcross, & Diclemente, 1994), and it marks the point at which a person is fully engaged, committed, and living out her new mindsets and habits that are necessary to achieve and maintain her goals. You've probably already been taking some new action steps all along, but the key now is to stay motivated with your actions, so that you continue to work towards the accomplishment of your goals. Everything that you have learned thus far is important to your success of staying in action. During the momentum stage, you need to keep applying all the tools that you've learned thus far.

Time management becomes very important to stay on track and to maximize the amount of momentum you have with your goals. Here are ten time-management tips to squeeze the most out of your calendar, and to be more productive than ever.

TIME MANAGEMENT TIPS TO INCREASE YOUR MOMENTUM

1. Daily "To-Do" Lists

The beauty of having broken down all your goals and actions into their smallest components is that it makes it really easy to fit these actions into your daily schedule. Simply refer to your list of steps and decide what you want to accomplish for the next day. Having several small tasks on your daily to-do list will not be overwhelming, and it will be easy to implement. If you can get into the habit of making a to-do list the night before, then all your days will be very productive.

2. Baby Steps and Milestones

The key to being able to consistently take action is to make sure that every action on your list is broken down into its smallest baby steps. Essentially, what you are doing is creating short-term goals. This will ensure that you are always clear on what your next steps are, and you are less likely to be overwhelmed. Research shows that short-term goals as opposed to long-term goals create higher levels of motivation (Locke & Latham, 1990), probably because we receive positive reinforcement and a sense of accomplishment quickly. So, get in the habit of breaking those big or long-term goals into easily achievable tasks.

3. Match Your Time and Energy

A big part of effectively managing time involves having enough energy to do what is required. There is a saying that we should manage our energy in addition to our time. For instance, which tasks do you find the most enjoyable or the easiest? Try saving these tasks for when your energy levels are low. This allows you to still get things done despite not feeling in the mood, because the actual task is something you like doing, or doesn't zap too much energy out of you. A classic example is the task of responding to emails. They are often easy and enjoyable. As a result, one might find it easiest to do this at the end of the day, as it doesn't require much brain power or stamina.

Likewise, think about which of your tasks are the least enjoyable, the most difficult, or require a great deal of concentration? Try to schedule these tasks for when your energy levels are at their peak. For instance, I know that when I have to do a lot of writing, I usually like to get this done during the beginning hours of the day when my mind is the most clear.

4. Seal the Deal!

Make a deal with yourself and commit to working on one of your tasks for a set period of time. Once that period of time passes, you can give yourself permission to quit. This strategy works well, because it builds momentum, and often you'll want to continue further past the original time commitment. It also takes the pressure off having to fully complete a task that might in turn decrease the quality of the outcome. In other words, you can focus on quality of work, rather than racing to finish the entire task or project within a set period of time.

5. Time and Energy Expanders

Identify those activities that actually seem to increase the amount of time and energy that you have to get things done. By investing our time and energy in the right activities, we can actually benefit. For example, what tasks get your energy moving the most? I can remember one of my clients telling me that over the one-month period when she had to create her business and marketing plan, she could only get focused and motivated by first doing a half-hour of cleaning in the morning. For her, it was a way to get her body moving and her mind warmed up. It also increased her sense of well-being, knowing that her environment was creating a sense of calm and inner peace for her.

Sometimes, women resort to cutting out certain activities that actually fuel their energy and inspiration to get things done. For instance, if you consider yourself to be a social or extraverted personality, then you want to make sure that you don't remove these positive interactions with people from your schedule. Often, these interactions keep us positive and full of energy. This means we're more likely to stay focused on the tasks that we value the most.

I've had people ask me how I find time to go to the gym four times a week, as they are bewildered at how I can fit that in along with all my other commitments. For me, when I do make the time to go, I actually end up having more energy and a better attitude towards my goals. This helps me stay on track and committed to taking my needed action steps.

6. The Power of Three, Two, or One!

Whenever I'm feeling really fatigued or lacking motivation and feeling pressured for time, I always remind myself of the "the power of three." This personal motto would inspire me to complete just three easy or simple actions towards one of my goals. It didn't matter how simple the tasks were, because what was more important was getting something done, as opposed to nothing. It is also another great way to create momentum in your day when you're feeling sluggish. Alternatively, you can use "the power of two" or "the power of one" depending on the amount of time you have. For instance, if you're on your lunch hour, you might just choose one task to complete. If it's a Saturday afternoon, you might choose three items.

7. Pareto Principle

According to the Pareto Principle, you can achieve 80 percent of your results through 20 percent of your efforts. The key is to identify what these few efforts are, and then to focus on them. For every goal, ask yourself, "What tasks are going to give me the greatest results?" Get in the habit of asking yourself, "What tasks or actions are unnecessary or irrelevant to this goal?" It's another way to simplify your processes towards achieving your goals.

8. Control Your Fear Factor

As we tackle different goals, we inevitably run into different tasks that require a certain amount of courage, because we fear taking the necessary actions. What is it that you fear? In terms of managing your time, try tackling this fear first. For some people, it might be getting a worrisome phone call or conversation out of the way. For others, it might be having to get their body fat measured. Whatever the fearful tasks are, try getting them out of the way first. This will free up your valuable energy to get other tasks completed.

9. Clean and Declutter Your Office or Desk Space

Clean your office or work space and be sure to declutter your surrounding environment. Otherwise, you'll lose valuable time searching for items and you'll also become distracted with your surroundings. It's amazing how much more productive we can become when our desks and offices are well organized.

10. Rise and Shine!

The rise and shine approach involves getting up early in the morning to complete some of your most important tasks. Not only are you less likely to be interrupted by others and phone calls, you might have more concentration as well. In addition, it can really bolster your self-confidence to have achieved so much, when most people are just starting their day. Give it a shot!

HOW DO I STAY ENGAGED OVER THE LONG TERM?

Have you ever come close to achieving a goal, and then started to lose motivation? As you reach the fifth stage of goal-setting achievement, which I refer to as *engagement,* you need to find ways to keep yourself engaged and motivated. In the original Stage of Change Model, they refer to this stage of change as *maintenance* (Prochaska, Norcross, & Diclemente, 1994), because it involves maintaining the results you've achieved, and not "falling off the wagon." I call this the art of engagement. It truly is an art, because staying motivated is something we need to constantly focus on to be successful. We all need regular boosts of motivation to maintain our efforts and actions.

At this stage of engagement, it is wise to continue reviewing the reasons you are maintaining your efforts, so you don't fall back into your old habits and ways of thinking that weren't conducive to your success. Remember, just because you have achieved your goal, or are close to it, it doesn't mean you won't sabotage your success and efforts. Continue to keep a journal and write down new habits and ways of thinking. Keep track of what's working and not working. Maintaining your success and staying engaged is all about staying motivated. Here are some of my top motivational tips to ensure you stay engaged with your goal-setting efforts.

MOTIVATION TIPS TO STAY ENGAGED

1. Personal Development

Keep feeding your mind with great sources of personal development resources. This is motivating because it's akin to always having a coach on hand to guide and inspire you, and remind you of what's important. Personal development comes in many shapes and forms:

- Nonfiction self-help books or "how to guides"
- Audio programs (Mp3 files) or audio books
- Attend local seminars and workshops on success-related topics
- Inspiring movies related to achieving success

These are just a few ways to keep your personal development in full gear. I guarantee that if you feed your mind with such positive and constructive messages regularly, you'll keep up your momentum and stay engaged with your goal-setting efforts.

2. Journalling

Journalling opens up new realms of possibility and new ways of thinking. It is a great way to solve motivational problems or other barriers that we might run into along the way. It is a great tool for self-expression and promotes self-awareness, which is what we need when it comes to learning how to motivate ourself. Often, journalling helps us to reconnect with our inner self and get connected to what matters the most to us. Writing allows us to get our thoughts out of our heads and onto paper, so that we can deal with barriers, problems, or plateaus in our motivation. Give it a shot to see how it can work wonders for you!

3. Plan a Reward or Celebration

Simply knowing that you'll give yourself a reward is something that can be motivating to work towards. Your rewards can be very basic or grander. For instance, if one of your small goals includes cleaning out your garage, then you might decide to reward yourself with a simple pleasure in life, such as a coffee from your favourite café or a dinner out with a friend. Maybe you'll take time to soak in a hot bathtub when you're finished. Alternatively, once you achieve a big goal, what will you reward yourself with? Maybe you'll finally allow yourself to go on a trip that you've always wanted, or you'll allow yourself to buy a few brand new outfits.

Speaking of the achievement of important life goals, I have learned that a lot of people seem to default towards the attitude that they don't need rewards or prizes and that they don't need to celebrate their successes. There is a powerful benefit to acknowledging your achievements. When you celebrate a really important achievement, you are integrating that experience into your self-concept and it enhances your self-esteem. It allows you to come to terms with the "new you," and it gives you the chance to reflect on how your life might be different and improved as a result of integrating this new accomplishment into your life. In other words, it prevents you from minimizing the achievement of your goals. If you can train your brain to associate positivity with your accomplishments, it only makes sense that you'll be motivated to accomplish even more with your life. So, be sure to use this motivational technique.

4. Play Music

If you're feeling sluggish and need the perfect "pick me up," playing music might be the best thing for you. Whether it's the latest tunes off the radio, or something classical and inspiring, you'll want to learn the effects that different types of music can have on your spirits and moods. Try different ethnic music, classical, instrumental, and so forth. Music gives us a new experiential perspective that can help us "get on with it."

5. What Makes You Feel Like a Million Bucks?

What are the activities in life that simply make you so happy that you feel like "a million bucks"? Does it involve going to the hairdresser once a month, getting your nails fancied up, visiting one of your inspirational friends regularly, or sitting on your porch with a cup of tea to reflect? What are the simple pleasures in life that you need to indulge in? It's different for everybody, but the key is to identify the activities that always seem to put the spark back in your step. When people are happy, they are more likely to be motivated and to put forth the effort in the things that matter the most to them. Make your own list.

6. Surround Yourself with Like-minded People

The more you surround yourself with people who have similar goals and a positive attitude, the more motivated you'll be to stay on track with your own goals. Having conversations with these people will remind you to stay focused on your big goals, and it will help ensure that you're taking the necessary action steps to move forward. Who are your friends and family members who give you that "feel-good" jolt of inspiration and motivation? Who are the ones who are striving to meet their own goals and reaching out of their comfort zone to do something much larger than themselves?

7. Create an Inspiring Work Sanctuary

Wherever you spend the bulk of your time doing your work and planning to achieve your goals, you'll want to make sure that your space is welcoming and motivational in nature. This is different for everyone. The point is that you want to feel very comfortable and "at home" in this space, because you'll be more productive, creative, and inspired about working on your goals. I've always had an obsession with beautiful office accessories, such as nice clocks, pens, and coasters. What objects do you find inspiring? I also love having beautiful arrangements of flowers and silk plants. Others need an office space with lots of light, or a really large desk. Some people choose to decorate their walls with artwork or prints that inspire them to hold onto their values. It is different for everyone. What can you do to your work space, so that it keeps you motivated?

AUTOMATE YOUR SUCCESS

The final stage of goal-setting achievement is *automaticity*. In the original Stage of Change Model, they refer to it as *termination* (Prochaska, Norcross, & Diclemente, 1994), which is described as the point in time at which an individual no longer has to exert effort or pay much attention to her new change. When you reach this stage, the changes that you've made are experienced as automatic, and there is no sense of ever slipping back to your old ways. This is often an ideal, but it's always worth striving for. With your goal setting and achievement efforts, you will know when you have arrived, because you will feel like you have learned how to automate your success. Your new beliefs, habits, and efforts will become natural, and you won't need to think about it as much as you used to. The truth is that to maintain and achieve our goals will always require a constant investment of our time, efforts, or energy. While this is the case, eventually, a person can reach a point where her investment of time and effort *seems* effortless and easy. Reaching the stage of automaticity is all about perfecting the processes that work for you. Continue to keep track in your journal of what is working. Continue seeking improvement and never give up on your big goals.

As you continue down your path to achieving your goals, you are inevitably going to run into different types of barriers. This can happen during any of the stages of goal-setting achievement. What can you do when this happens?

OVERCOMING INEVITABLE BARRIERS

Sometimes, we are our own worst enemy when we attempt to achieve our big goals. We are constantly putting up blocks, so that we can't move forward. Running into barriers is completely normal, but you must be aware of this. Otherwise, you'll take your barriers too seriously. Barriers can be experienced in many different ways, including the following:

- Roadblocks
- Uncertainty
- Dead-ends
- Stalling
- Finding all the problems in a situation
- Mistakes and failures
- Paralysis (due to fear or something else)
- Overanalyzing a situation

- Unsure of which decision or path to suddenly take
- Not having enough information to move forward
- Sabotage
- A sense of something being too risky

Do any of the above sound familiar? I know they're familiar to me. All of the above are different ways that we experience barriers and roadblocks. The key is to become aware of which roadblocks keep getting in your way. With this awareness, you can prepare plans for how to overcome them.

Often, our barriers are a reflection of the limiting beliefs that we hold about a situation. For instance, I once met a successful businesswoman who had only a high school education. One of her emerging dreams was to become a life coach, but she believed that she would need to go back to school to get several degrees, in order to accomplish this goal. I asked her why she wouldn't take a coaching certification course, and she told me that no one would hire a coach who didn't have a formal education. In this case, I had to work with my client to ask her why she was putting this roadblock up herself. Clearly, she did not need formal degrees, in order to start her coaching business. After my client realized that she had created her own roadblock, she actually started her coaching business without any certification. Sometimes, our barriers are things that we create without realizing it.

Other times, we run into roadblocks that really do require a lot more problem solving. This is inevitable. Therefore, we must prepare for this to happen. As I mentioned in the beginning, the more you plan ahead, the stronger your foundation is for achieving your goal. Any goal worth achieving is going to have "obstacles" that need to be overcome. Otherwise, everyone would have achieved their goals by now.

If you can think of ways to handle your barriers ahead of time, then you greatly increase your chances of overcoming your barriers and problems.

Let's consider the goal of learning to set stronger boundaries, i.e., having more time to oneself within close relationships. Often, these individuals are simply stuck for what words or language to use when stating that they need time alone. If this were your goal, you would brainstorm a list of statements that you could use when "caught" in an uncomfortable situation. This would increase the chances of overcoming the barrier of not being able to speak up and set healthy boundaries. The great thing about planning ahead in this case is that you can *individualize* what you are going to *say* or *do* when you encounter obstacles or sticky situations. The important point is that you find what works for you and what you are most comfortable with.

Dealing with barriers and obstacles is nothing more than creative problem solving in which a solution is put into action. But you can't put anything into action if you haven't brainstormed a solution that will work for *you*.

In your journal, record a list of the barriers that you anticipate you will face. Then, write down ideas of how you will address these barriers.

HELP, I'M STUCK! A FOUR-STEP ACTION PLAN

Have you ever had the experience that no matter what you try, you can never seem to reach your goal? I think we've all been there at some point in time. Let me encourage you to *not* give up. There is always a way to make it happen. It's just about finding the best way that will work for you.

The first step is to simply get clear on what has *not worked* for you in the past. This list might also surprise you when you find out that you haven't actually tried as many approaches as you thought. This list is useful, because it will prevent you from "banging your head against the wall," where you keep on trying the same, or slightly different approaches, that don't work for you. You think, "Maybe this time, I'll have the discipline to make it happen." But after you try and it fails to work, you are not surprised. So, stop putting yourself through this cycle.

Secondly, what could you try? Take a good hour of your time to focus on this question alone. What are other possible solutions that you haven't considered before? Write down all your options even if you think they won't work. Then, ask yourself, "If I were to try to make this option work, what would I need to do?" In other words, you're trying on "what-if" scenarios.

The third step is to consider contacting a professional with expertise related to your goal. For instance, if your goal is to become a professional speaker, consider hiring a consultant or coach who can help you with this.

Finally, consider finding a mentor or role model. A mentor is someone who usually has expertise and experience related to your own goal pursuits. Talk to as many people as you can who have achieved a goal that is similar in nature to your own. Ask for their recommendations and guidance, and ask for introductions to other professionals who might be able to help you.

CHAPTER 13

Secrets for Staying Focused and Following Through

A BRAND NEW CHAPTER BEGINS

I believe that a whole new chapter is about to open in your life. My hope is that you have gleaned several new insights from reading this book and completing the action steps within.

I encourage you to complete any of the exercises that you haven't already completed, and to repeat all of the exercises with your other life goals. This is a system that you can apply to any goal in your life. I also encourage you to start your own journal or binder where you can reflect on what you've learned while reading this book and completing the exercises. What do you know now that you didn't know before? How does this information fit in with what you've previously learned from reading other books or attending seminars? What will you need to return to for further review?

Be sure to mark the pages that you need to return to, and then schedule a time to review them. Otherwise, you'll forget to return to the book, and you may forget some of the important insights that you've learned.

Before wrapping up this final chapter, there are a few other points worth sharing with you. Here they are: believe in yourself, be patient and persistent, and finally, don't let your fears hold you back.

1. HAVE FAITH IN YOURSELF!

One of the greatest things about exercising your personal faith is that you don't have to get permission from anyone to do it. Your faith is already inside you, waiting for you to lean on it, exercise it, and trust it. Think of faith as being like a muscle—the more you use it, the stronger it will become. If you are currently not happy with where you are in your life, and you want to achieve something different or more, then you will need to exercise your muscle of faith. Exercising our faith is what brings us from one level of accomplishment to another. It's what keeps a person taking baby steps, as opposed to no steps at all. In order to make all of your dreams come true, regardless of whether or not you know *how to* at this exact moment in time, you will need to believe in yourself. I have found that faith is what keeps us going, when times are tough and we feel like giving up.

How do you get to the point where you can truly believe in yourself? This is, of course, easier said than done. In part, it stems from being aligned with your true passions. When you know exactly what you are passionate about doing, you will feel *compelled* to set out to achieve the corresponding goals. We must get in the habit of focusing on the value that we are bringing to ourself, other people, and the world at large. In the words of Marrianne Williamson, "Your playing small does not serve the world." Just remember, often it is helpful to get in touch with the "why" behind your goals. We all have unique reasons, and we must learn to place importance on these reasons. Your passion, talent, and goals are unique and different from anyone else's. This is special, whether you believe it or not. If you want to carry your ambitions out to the world, you must be the one to believe in yourself before anyone else.

Try mustering up the self-talk that everything will work out just fine. You might not know *how* you're going to make your dreams happen in detail, but it's empowering to *believe* that somehow they will happen if you put forth all the effort you have. We must trust that things will unfold positively. Exercising this faith gives us comfort and provides a bridge of support for our anxiety during uncertain times in life. This is one of the most critical factors in becoming successful.

Sometimes, we can lose confidence and not believe in ourself when we don't have a plan that is guaranteed or when we don't have a precise map for where we are headed. Eventually, we will figure out these details, but we must realize that clarity for a particular goal is a process that unfolds with time, effort, learning, and of course, some trial and error. In order to succeed, it is not necessary to know every single detail of how we'll achieve our goals. Women who become successful know this ahead of time, and they don't let the uncertainty of their circumstances hold them back. Eventually, with continued effort and action, we'll find many different paths, resources, and people who will enable us to achieve our dreams. We just need to trust our own individual process and realize that we are doing the best we can with the knowledge that we currently have.

2. PERSISTENCE AND PATIENCE

You may be putting a lot of time into something in your life, and feeling as though you're not getting the results that you expected. During these times, it is wise to persist and continue taking baby steps whenever possible. The delays that we experience are not necessarily denials. When we believe in the importance of what we are doing and that it could be appreciated by the world, it is easier for us to persist. If you keep putting forth your best efforts, eventually, you are going to get something back in return.

Sometimes in life, it takes a lot of "invisible work" or efforts that cannot be readily observed by others before we finally experience any visible results. Walt Disney went bankrupt several times before he created and opened Disney World. What would have happened if he had given up? He knew that his defeat was only temporary and that he must persist. If you study any truly successful person, you will learn that he or she went through many tough times and experienced much discouragement.

3. FACE YOUR FEARS

Whatever it is with respect to your goals that you fear, there is one thing to remember: Embrace your fear and work through it. The only way fear goes away is by facing it. Think about the first time you were about to dive off a diving board. Were you scared? How did you get yourself to leap forward and dive? You confronted the fear by simply allowing yourself to feel the fear while you dove. The more we end up doing something that we fear, the easier it will be, and the less fear we will have.

As a child, we seldom let fear hold us back. We took risks like learning how to ride a bicycle, swimming without our water wings, deciding to join our siblings for the first time on an upside-down rollercoaster, entering a haunted house, and so on. As a child, we still had fear, but we were in the habit of embracing and understanding our fear as a natural progression in growing up and achieving maturity. As adults, we try to avoid fear as often as possible. We try to trick ourself and tell ourself that we will be okay if we just stay inside our comfort zone. Some people would rather look good and be right, than take a risk in life. Unfortunately, these are the people who seldom lead rich and fulfilling lives. The world has a way of rewarding those who face their fears and take action. If we can realize that fear is a natural part of achieving our goals, we can more easily approach our fears with less anxiety.

Whatever you fear most, it is your fear that has the power.
-Oprah Winfrey

The key is to manage our fears and not let them overwhelm or paralyze us. Just as it is important to break a large goal into small baby steps, the same is true for dealing with our fears. We can begin facing our fears by chipping away at small components of those overwhelming tasks, events, or situations that cause us fear. We can start where it is easiest, by facing a small component of our fear. Keep going, and take baby steps. You'll get stronger. As you take more action, you'll gain more confidence.

It is worth repeating. Don't get caught in the trap where you have to have the whole plan together before you do anything. If everyone were to wait until they felt they "had it all together," they'd be waiting a long time. They might never take action. This is the reason so many people don't achieve their full potential. They don't take any action, because they don't believe they are ready.

Being ready has a preparation and planning component, however, it is also a state of mind. Successful people don't wait until things are perfect before they begin. They just begin. Begin anywhere. Even if you begin in the wrong spot, don't worry. The world has a way of letting you know, based on feedback that you will receive. But, the universe can't provide you with any feedback or give you any help until you begin to help yourself. To that end, what is one thing that you want to pursue or take action with? Decide today to take one small step closer to your dream. Maybe it's a phone call. Maybe its researching some information. Whatever it is, take one action. As you take this action step, you'll automatically create further momentum with your success!

Life is either a daring adventure or nothing at all.
-Helen Keller

By exercising your faith, being persistent, and learning to face your fears, you won't be able to help but move forward in your life.

REFERENCES

Canfield, J. (2005). *The Success Principles: How to get from where you are to where you want to be*. New York: HarperCollins Publishers.

Dunkel, C. S., Kelts, D, & Coon, B. (2006). Possible Selves as Mechanisms of Change in Therapy. In C. Dunkel & J. Kerpelman (Eds.), *Possible Selves: Theory, Research and Application* (187-204). New York: Nova Science Publishers, Inc.

Kayes, D. C. (2005). The destructive pursuit of idealized goals. *Organizational Dynamics, 34*(4), 391-401.

Kayes, D. C. (2006). *Destructive Goal Pursuit: The Mount Everest Disaster*. New York: Palgrave MacMillan Ltd.

King, L. A., & Burton, C. M. (2003). The Hazards of Goal Pursuit. In E. C. Chang & L. J. Sanna (Eds.), *Virtue, Vice, and Personality: The Complexity of Behavior*. (pp. 53-69). Washington, DC: American Psychological Association.

Koestner, R. (2008). Reaching one's personal goals: A motivational perspective focused on autonomy. *Canadian Psychology, 49*(1), 60-67.

Latham, G. P. (2004). The motivational benefits of goal-setting. *Academy of Management Executive, 18*(4), 126-129.

Latham, G. P., & Locke, E. A. (2006). Enhancing the benefits and overcoming the pitfalls of goal setting. *Organizational Dynamics, 35*(4), 332-340.

Latham, G. P. & Locke, E. A. (2007). New developments in and directions for goal-setting research. *European Psychologist, 12*(4), 290-300.

Locke, E. A., & Latham, G. P. (1984). *Goal Setting: A Motivational Technique that Works!* Englewood Cliffs, NJ: Prentice-Hall, Inc.

Locke, E. A. & Latham, G. P. (1990). *A theory of goal setting and task performance.* Englewood Cliffs, NJ: Prentice Hall.

Locke, E. A. & Latham, G. P. (2002). Building a practically useful theory of goal setting and task motivation. A 35 year odyssey. *American Psychologist, 57*(9), 705-717.

Losier, M. (2003). *The Law of Attraction: The science of attracting more of what you want and less of what you don't.* Victoria, BC: Michael J. Losier.

Markus, H., & Nurius, P. (1986). Possible selves. *American Psychologist, 41*(9), 954-969.

Mitchell, K. E., Levin, A. S., & Krumboltz, J. D. (1999). Planned happenstance: Constructing unexpected career opportunities. *Journal of Counseling and Development, 77,* 115-124.

Muraven, M. & Baumeister, R. F. (2000). Self regulation and depletion of limited resources: does self control resemble a muscle? *Psychology Bulletin,126,* 247-259.

Ordonez, L. D., Schweitzer, M. E., Galinksy, A. D., & Bazerman, M. H. (2009). Goals gone wild: The systematic side effects of over-prescribing goal setting. *Harvard Business School, Working Paper 09-083,* 1-26.

Pavlina, S. (2009). *Personal development for smart people: The conscious pursuit of personal growth.* USA: Hay House Publishing.

Polivy, J., & Herman, P. C. (2002). If at first you don't succeed: False hopes of self-change [Electronic version]. *American Psychologist, 57*(9), 677-689.

Prochaska, J. O., Norcross, J. C., & Diclemente, C. C. (1994). *Changing for good: A revolutionary six-stage program for overcoming bad habits and moving your life positively forward.* HarperCollins, New York.

Robbins, A. (1991). Awaken the Giant Within: How to take immediate control of your mental, physical, and financial destiny. New York: Simon & Schuster, Inc.

Schachter, H. (Monday, April 26, 2010). Forget SMART goals; go for the hard ones. [Electronic Version]. Retrieved from Globe & Mail: http://www.theglobeandmail.com/report-on-business/managing/morning-manager/forget-smart-goals-go-for-the-hard-ones/article1546926/

Schack, T., Whitmarsh, B., Pike, R., & Redden, C. (2005). Goal Setting. In J. Taylor & G. Wilson (Eds.). *Applying Sports Psychology: Four Perspectives.* (pp.137-150). U.S.A.: Human Kinetics.

Weinburg, R. S., Harmison, R. J., Rosenkranz, R., & Hookom, S. (2005). Goal Setting. In J. Taylor & G. Wilson (Eds.). *Applying Sports Psychology: Four Perspectives.* (pp.101-116). U.S.A.: Human Kinetics.